JUBILATION

THE UNBROKEN CIRCLE SERIES

THE UNBROKEN CIRCLE SERIES links Ancient African Christianity with the African American experience. The common bond is the "sad joyfulness" which permeates both. The series curates timely themes from the Fellowship of St. Moses the Black annual conferences with other essays by leaders and friends of the Fellowship.

Also from the Unbroken Circle Press:

THE UNBROKEN CIRCLE SERIES
VOLUME TWO

JUBILATION
CULTURES OF SACRED MUSIC

*"Linking ancient African Christianity
with the African American experience"*

NUN KATHERINE WESTON
SERIES EDITOR

KEVIN BRYCE
ASSOCIATE EDITOR

Fellowship of St. Moses the Black
Unbroken Circle Press

FSMB 2022

"American Orthodox Music: Towards a Synthesis" was published in the original version in *By the Waters: Selected Works by Students of St. Tikhon's Orthodox Theological Seminary,* No. 7, © 2008. It has been updated and published here by the kind permission of the seminary and the author.

"The Canon for Racial Reconciliation" © 2007 by Sts. Cosmas & Damian Bookstore, PO Box 1887, Anniston, AL 36202-1887. panteleimonmd@aol.com. This canon has been revised and used by permission.

FRONT COVER: Icon of St. Moses the Black painted for Unbroken Circle Press.

Printed on demand.

Published by the Brotherhood of St. Moses the Black under the imprint Unbroken Circle Press
P.O. Box 88442
Indianapolis IN 46208

ubcp@mosestheblack.org

PUBLISHER'S CATALOGING–IN-PUBLICATION DATA

Names: Weston, Nun Katherine, editor. | Bryce, Kevin, editor. |
                Fellowship of St. Moses the Black, sponsoring body.
Title: Jubilation : cultures of sacred music / Nun Katherine
                Weston, series editor ; Kevin Bryce, associate editor.
Description: Indianapolis, Indiana : Unbroken Circle Press, 2022. | Series:
                The Unbroken Circle series ; v. 2. | "Linking ancient African
                Christianity with the African American experience." |
                Includes bibliographical references.
Identifiers: ISBN: 978-1-7354895-2-0
Subjects: LCSH: Spirituals (Songs) | Gospel music. | African Americans
                —Music. | Sacred songs. | Sacred music. | Church music. |
                Music—Religious aspects—Christianity. | African Americans
                — Religion. | Orthodox Eastern Church—Songs and music.
Classification: LCC: ML3556 .J83 2022 | DDC: 780.89/96073—dc23

BE JUBILANT, MY SOUL

Praise Him with tuneful cymbals,
Praise Him with cymbals of jubilation.
Let every breath praise the Lord.

—Psalm 150:5, 6

JUBILEE

Jubilee, jubilee—
    O, my Lord.
Early in de mornin',
    My Lord, jubilee!
Shout, my children, you are free!
    O, my Lord.
My God brought you liberty.
    My Lord, jubilee!

Call me Sunday Christian,
    O, my Lord.
Call me Monday devil,
    My Lord, jubilee!
Don't care what you call me,
    O, my Lord.
My Jesus loves me!
    My Lord, jubilee!

—Gullah-Geechee Ring Shout*

---

* A "ring shout" is an African American religious song accompanied by a counterclockwise shuffling walk, used after the main church services are over. The McIntosh County Shouters are the last group to keep the unbroken tradition alive.

THIS BOOK IS GRATEFULLY DEDICATED:

To Fr. Moses Berry, President Emeritus
of the Fellowship of St. Moses the Black,
who unfailingly reminds us to remember our roots
and to *abide in the vine* (Jn 15:4).

And to Fr. Jerome Sanderson, founding member
who has enriched our conferences
with his love of music and of the African Saints.

CONTENTS

II MUSICALITY

III FROM THE FIELD

APPENDICES

INTRODUCTION

MUSIC OF A SUFFERING PEOPLE

DR. CARLA THOMAS

I T IS MY PRIVILEGE AND PLEASURE to introduce you to this second volume in the Unbroken Circle Series, dedicated to our prayerful experience of music. The essays curated here all reflect on African American worship music from an Orthodox Christian worldview. The Orthodox tradition, going back over two thousand years is difficult to define, but not difficult to share experientially. As a mother of three (and now a grandmother!) I have had to develop a method to communicate this understanding, and I would like to share it with you. To begin, I have the children spell the word Orthodoxy, then I give them this acrostic—

- **O** represents the Original Christian religion.
- **R** is for Religious purity and the attainment and preservation of it. There were seven Ecumenical Councils during the first thousand years of the Church in order to delineate and define the dogmas of the Church.
- **T** stands for the Theotokos which means the Bearer of God, the Mother of God. She is also referred to as the

Ever-virgin Mary. Among the Protestant denominations which formed centuries later, Mary lost much of her significance; however, in Orthodoxy she is viewed as the Queen of Heaven, and Ever-virgin, as she had no subsequent children.

- **H** stands for the Holy Mysteries of the Church. These are Baptism, Chrismation, Eucharist, Confession, Unction, Marriage, and Ordination. These are the primary sacraments which we in the Orthodox Church hold as holy.*
- **O** stands for Odes to saints and angels. As an illustration I would like to share one of my favorite Helen Keller moments.†

Many years ago, I was providing medical care for an inmate at a correctional facility. As I waited for his chart, I noticed he was reading a book on the subject of angels. I asked if I could see the book and he was agreeable. After passing me the book the inmate said, "This tells you all about angels." To which I replied, "Oh, does it tell you the ranks of angels?" He said, "No." I then told him about the ranks of angels and what St. Paul said about them, the seraphim, cherubim, thrones, dominions, principalities, powers, and so forth. He said, "Okay." Then I said, "Can you name the archangels?" He said, "Sure, Michael and Gabriel." To which I replied, "Did you know there are eight of them?" I could sense that I was losing him when he said, "Well, that's not in the Bible." I conceded the point then followed up by saying that in the fullness of Christianity, not all of the Traditions of the Church are in the Bible. I then asked, "Do you believe there is an archangel named Raphael, the angel of healing?" He said, "Yeah, that's

---

* The Holy Mysteries are the visible means by which the faithful receive the invisible Grace of God. While seven Holy Mysteries are typically enumerated, by no means is this meant to place a limit on the action of the Uncreated Grace of God.

† Helen Keller's early loss of sight and hearing frustrated her development of speech. Her teacher helped her connect the sensation of water with an early speech memory, sparking the understanding that things have names that can be spoken and signed.

true." I said, "Is that in the Bible?" At that moment I knew I had him!* That was the Helen Keller moment, because in that moment he realized that he did not possess the fullness of Christianity. That is the beauty of Orthodoxy; it is the fullness of Christianity. Now back to the acrostic for Orthodoxy:

- **D** stands for Dogma. When I speak to my children about this point, I tell them about the Holy Trinity, Father, Son, and Holy Spirit. I also tell them of the trinity of holy acts: almsgiving, fasting, and prayer.

When the Western Christian confessions did away with the art and discipline of fasting in an attempt to make it easier for people to come to Christ, they actually lost large numbers of people. In prisons, one of the arguments used against the cause of Christ is the lack of fasting. When I encounter this erroneous belief, I correct it and let inmates know that if they go back to the beginning of Church history, they will find that the discipline of fasting was at the center of the spiritual life of each believer.

A number of years ago, the Baptist church, which I also attended, introduced a four-hour fast to the community. I said that's good; let's do it every week, let's keep doing it. I believe that increasingly Christians of all stripes are realizing that we cannot purify our souls without ascetical labor, and part of that labor, which anyone can do, is fasting. Not everyone will die for Christ like St. Ignatius,† but all of us can fast.

- **O** stands for Oil. I am a physician, so of course I had to add a spiritual-medicine aspect to the definition,—the Golden Rule (see Mt 7:12), the Ten Commandments (see Exo 20:2–17), the Nine Beatitudes (see Mt 5:3–12).

---

* The names of the Archangels are as follows: Barachiel, Jegudiel, Selaphiel, Uriel, Raphael, Jeremiel, Michael, and Gabriel. The story of Raphael is in the book of Tobit, in the Apocrypha.

† St. Ignatius of Antioch, also known as the God-Bearer, was instructed in the faith by the Apostles and served as an early bishop of Antioch. Additionally, according to tradition, he was the child whom our Lord held and blessed (see Mt 18:2–4). St. Ignatius is considered one of the Apostolic Fathers and suffered martyrdom at Rome in the year 108 A.D.

We also talk about podvig,* suffering, and unceasing prayer—"Lord Jesus Christ, Son of God, have mercy upon me a sinner."

- **X** stands for Xylophone, the music of the Church, which has been transmitted to us through the ages, some of which were given to the Orthodox Church through angelic encounters.
- **Y** is for St. Andrew's cross (use your imagination here—it actually looks like an "X"). If you look at the flag for the State of Alabama you will see an example of St. Andrew's cross. If you tilt it back up, it's the sign of the cross in the familiar orientation.

We make this sign with the first three fingers joined together, and the remaining two fingers pressed against the palm. Then we touch our forehead, chest, right then left shoulders saying, Glory to the Father, and to the Son, and to the Holy Spirit. The preceding was only a brief outline of Orthodoxy but, God willing, it has provided a common framework to help us reflect on the African American worship music that will be the focus of this volume.

IN A LAND where the pursuit of earthly happiness is the common goal, there survives a collection of songs which speak to a spiritual disposition which runs counter to the norm. These songs are known as Spirituals, "jubilee songs," "sorrow songs," and "joy songs." These hymns were created and sung by people who knew there was a heavenly homeland where there was neither bond nor free (cf. Gal 3:28). Just as with other folk music traditions there is no identifiable author; we know that Spirituals contain elements that are both African and European in nature.

The European element is what we could describe as a jewel, seen in a glass darkly (cf. 1 Cor 13:12). The jewel which

---

* "Podvig" is the Slavic term for spiritual struggle.

the enslavers gave to the enslaved was that of Christianity. I'm not sure they understood how powerful that action was, because even though it was obscured by a great evil, even though it was imperfectly practiced by those who delivered it, even though it was not the fullness of the faith, it still planted a seed in their hearts. And in time this gem shone so brightly that it brought us to where we are today.

The combination of the African capacity for suffering and the seed of Christianity transmitted by the slaveholders in the heat of bondage, brought forth this flower called the Spiritual. Anyone can sing the Spiritual, but it is especially true for those who have suffered. You can feel the deep-rooted peace that comes through Spirituals. There are times when they are sung with joy. "This Little Light of Mine" is very joyful; but there are others which are able to articulate suffering felt deep within the soul when ordinary words may fail during times of crisis, trial, or tribulation. This is the purpose of the Spiritual.

Because of the depth of suffering and the height of joy which these songs express, they speak to the essence of having Christ's peace in our hearts, this peace which we find in Orthodoxy. The most important thing is that God, in His awesome, wonderful, mysterious way, became more real to the slaves than the hardship of enslavement, and that is a miracle. The reason the enslaved accepted Christianity was because Christ entered their hearts, and became an undeniable reality to those who embraced Him. Although the Christianity presented to them was neither full nor fully practiced, yet even through this glass darkly the brilliant reality of Christ shone. A baptism of suffering and repentance is key to both Orthodoxy and Spirituals.

Trust in God was the slaves' only hope, as it should be our only hope. An enslaver could sell the members of your family, and they could brand or maim you. They could make you work from what in Alabama is called "cain't see to cain't see," which means from before dawn to after dusk. We may be tempted to think that we are better off than they, but in some ways we fare worse. As Hieromonk Alexii has said, "The pressure is off." Still, we must continually strive to trust in God as our only hope.

Some enslavers allowed slaves to sit in the balcony during church services, while others forbade services altogether following the custom around schooling. This precipitated the emergence of invisible churches and whispering preachers. These were not unlike the Orthodox catacomb churches of early Christendom. To show trust in God and to surrender to Him, the slaves sang "I'm Troubled in Mind." A portion of the lyrics are as follows,

> I'm troubled, I'm troubled, I'm troubled in mind.
> If Jesus don't help me, I surely will die.*

As you can see, the slaves that composed and sang this song knew Jesus as their only hope. Another hymn, "We Are Climbing Jacob's Ladder," speaks of the constant struggle to reach God the Father, to know the Son, and to be visited by the Holy Ghost. If Christ had not been real to the slaves, they could not have composed such heart-rending songs. What came from the heart of God, reached the heart of the slaves, and all that had ears to hear.

The slaves sang "We Are Climbing Jacob's Ladder" to show that the struggle is lifelong and that it could be lost at any time. The ladder has an unknown height. For some it is short; for others it is very long. The rungs are virtues and ascetical labors, while trials, tribulations, temptation, and the passions are winds which seek to cause us to fall from the ladder, to Hades below.

---

* The following is a story from the period of enslavement related to this song: This Negro Spiritual was sung by a former slave known as Mrs. Brown, who learned the song from her father. She said that when he had been whipped, he would sit on a log outside their cabin and sing it with such pathos that even his masters were moved.

AN ADDITIONAL ASPECT of Spirituals which we have yet to address is their role in the Underground Railroad. For example, when Harriet Tubman would lead escaped slaves from house to house on their journey North towards the Ohio River, she would sometimes sing "Wade in the Water." The song was originally meant for baptism, but she adapted it to let the escaping Africans know to wade through the water to throw off the scent of the bloodhounds.[1]

"Steal Away" was another song used by the Underground Railroad. When Harriet Tubman or other conductors passed through an area and they began to sing, "Steal away, steal away, steal away to Jesus," it was a sign that the time to get on the train had come for all who were ready for freedom.

In addition to the multilayered meanings of the Spirituals, there are other aspects I'd like to briefly point out. This genre of music has what are called "Triple A" qualities—adaptability, accessibility, and availability. It is important to remember that Spirituals were composed and sung by a people who were forbidden to learn how to read or write, so generally they were simple in construction. However, that very same simplicity disguises the depth of meaning and power contained therein, and this is one of the wonderful aspects of their nature.* While ministering within prisons and nursing homes I have witnessed the value of this characteristic. For people who do not have access to hymnals or aren't able to see them, Spirituals serve as the perfect songs.

When we speak of adaptability, we mean that a singer may insert new phrases or even verses into a well-known song customizing it for the audience or occasion at hand without doing violence to the musical tradition. By accessibility we mean that one does not have to be literate to benefit from Spirituals. Finally, by availability we mean that regardless of how you're feeling or the crisis you are facing, when you learn enough of them, they will rest on your heart and provide comfort during times of tribulation.

---

* Likewise, many of the great writers of the Orthodox Faith had the gift of simplicity, so that the homilies could be understood by all who heard them.

I WANT TO REVISIT the topic of adaptability, because this allowed the Spirituals to adapt to the new life of the freedmen after emancipation. They were introduced to the public through stage performances, and adorned with new forms of harmony and instrumentation. But the Spirituals also adapted in church services to the new conditions the freedmen found themselves in, both in the Great Migration to the Northern and Western parts of the US, and for those who remained in the South. What emerged was Gospel music. And many black churches use a combination of Spirituals and Gospel in their service. To the visitor they might seem indistinguishable when the Spirituals are sung in the Gospel style.

Many Spirituals contain "blue notes." This means that the 3rd or 7th is flatted, giving the song a minor feel. This becomes more noticeable in the transition to Gospel. And, by the way, that minor quality is also part of Orthodox liturgical music, especially during Great Lent. During the Great Fast we convert choral responses to the minor key because those melodies inspire a sense of anguish and suffering as we refocus our attention on the need for repentance.

I WANT TO SHARE something about my own conversion experience to the Orthodox Faith. I was brought up on a particular style of musical expression, on what I have described above, and the loss of that during worship was difficult. In particular, the monotone chant used when reading the Psalter or other prayers was a very difficult adjustment; however, in time I have learned to adjust and see the benefit. By reading in this manner the text is universalized making it easier to digest by everyone present. That said, I will still welcome the emergence of Orthodox liturgical music that speaks to the soul weaned on Spirituals and Gospel music. And now I will introduce you to the contributors and their chapters, starting with myself.

I AM *Carla Newbern Thomas, MD*. In June 1988, I was welcomed into the Orthodox Church in Atlanta, Georgia. I drove 180 miles each week to attend St. John the Wonderworker. In 2006, some of my nursing home patients insisted that I take them to church. I realized that the time had come for me to put down Orthodox roots. I shyly called His Eminence Archbishop Dmitri (of blessed memory). Less than seven days later, to my surprise, he arrived at my office for evening prayers. Stamping his crozier on the waiting room floor, he planted the St. Luke Orthodox Mission Station on November 25, 2006. Our outreach is a free medical clinic, in partnership with the Fellowship of St. Moses the Black and the Saints Cosmas and Damian Society. I am also on the board of St. Vladimir's Orthodox Theological Seminary, Axia (Orthodox Women), and Orthodox Christian Prison Ministry. I have helped lead prayer times and hymn singing at Fellowship conferences from the time I started attending. The "Canon for Racial Reconciliation," (Appendix I) is one of the prayers we use in various Fellowship gatherings, and it is also used in prison ministry.

Hieromonk* Alexii Altschul is the superior of the Holy Archangel Michael and All Angels Skete in Weatherby, Missouri. Prior to his conversion to Orthodoxy, he and his wife helped found the Reconciliation Ministry on Troost Avenue in Kansas City, Missouri, which was the city's racial dividing line. He is a founding member of the Fellowship of St. Moses the Black, and currently serves as its Spiritual Advisor. His engaging chapter chronicles how he met and married his wife, known to the Orthodox world as Matushka† Michaila, and how Gospel music infused their relationship. He also speaks to the spirituality of African American worship music.

---

* A "hieromonk" is an Orthodox priest-monk.

† Matushka is a Russian term for a priest's wife; it is a diminutive form of "mother."

Fr. Deacon Jonathan Reavis is the Director of Programs for Lotus Care House, a housing navigation center that provides bridge housing for the chronically homeless in Kansas City, Missouri. In 2019, Jonathan was ordained to the holy diaconate in the Serbian Orthodox Church, and also joined the Board of the Fellowship of St. Moses the Black that same year. He has presented at a few of our annual conferences. Dn. Jonathan's chapter explores themes in the Spirituals, comparing their theology with that expressed in well-known Orthodox hymns. He uses, as a vantage point, his encounters with Spirituals in both Protestant and Orthodox settings, giving us an essay at once both scholarly and deeply personal.

Fr. Moses Berry, a retired Orthodox priest, is the founding pastor of Christ the Good Shepherd Orthodox Church in St. Louis, Missouri and of the Unexpected Joy Church in Ash Grove, Missouri. He is also the President Emeritus of the Fellowship of St. Moses the Black. He draws from his personal family history to show the deep, otherworldly Christianity that has been passed down from the righteous slaves who suffered in this country. He interweaves wisdom from the "old timers" who helped raise him with his personal experience of growing up on Gospel music in church. He also introduces us to the genesis and significance of that genre of worship music.

Fr. Damascene Christensen is the abbot of the St. Herman of Alaska Brotherhood in Northern California and author of *Father Seraphim Rose: His Life and Works.* He has presented on the topics of the Spirituals and Gospel music at several of our annual conferences. Here, he develops the theme of Gospel music and its resonances with the teachings of the Holy Fathers of the Church. He shares hymn texts side by side with patristic quotations. Through this he demonstrates the universality of the suffering Christian experience.

Fr. Deacon John R. Gresham, Jr. lives in King William County, Virginia where he served as a Baptist Pastor for 17 years before becoming Orthodox in 2014. He served on our Board for many years and also established the Virginia

Chapter of the Fellowship of St. Moses the Black. In 2018, he earned the St. Stephen's Certificate in Orthodox Theology from the Antiochian House of Studies. He recently authored *Become All Flame: Lent with African Saints,* released in 2022. Building on Fr. Damascene's presentation on Gospel music, Dn. John brings the spotlight on one particular Gospel singer, Dorothy Love Coates, in the context of his lifelong experience with that music.

Fr. Turbo Qualls is the rector at St. Mary of Egypt Serbian Orthodox Church in Kansas City, Missouri. He studied under the contemporary master iconographer, Fr. Stamatis Skliris of Athens, complementing that by completing the Antiochian House of Studies course in theology, with an emphasis in Iconology. Fr. Turbo served for many years as Dean of Chapters for the Fellowship, and has been a regular presenter at our conferences. Fr. Turbo's essay is derived from a homily he delivered to the St. Mary's choir in 2019. He shows us the correspondences between heavenly and earthly worship. From that, he convincingly argues that the weapon of prayer for the world, during the Divine Liturgy, is superior to any earthly strategy for this-worldly justice.

Hieromonk Andrew Wermuth is the superior of the St. Michael Skete on Spruce Island, Alaska—the island where St. Herman once lived. He joined the St. Herman of Alaska Brotherhood in 1995, subsequently attending St. Tikhon Seminary where he first wrote his essay "Orthodox Christian Music: Towards a Synthesis." It was published by St. Tikhon's in 2008 in *By the Waters.* It is reprinted here in updated form by the gracious permission of Archimandrite* Sergius, and with Fr. Andrew's collaboration. This important chapter looks at the precedent for using elements of regional folk music in liturgical composition. It further explores Appalachian folk music and Negro Spirituals as the best candidates to serve as musical inspiration for American Orthodox music.

---

* An "archimandrite" is a high-ranking priest-monk, and often the abbot of a monastery.

Nun Katherine Weston, Superior of St. Xenia Monastic Community in Indianapolis, Indiana, is a founding member and current president of the Fellowship of St. Moses the Black. She is also the general editor of the Fellowship's Unbroken Circle Press. To help support her monastery, she works as a licensed mental health counselor in private practice. Music has been a love and inspiration for her whole life. In the '90s she sang Spirituals and composed songs as part of her parish's Revelation Coffeehouse youth ministry. In 2005 she first began using the Spirituals as an inspiration for Orthodox liturgical composition. For this volume, she contributed three things: a "Postscript" to Fr. Andrew's article, bringing it up to date with the liturgical composers currently using "Americana" folk elements. Next, she offers a brief history of the development of Spirituals and Gospel music. And finally, a reflection on her own compositional process in hopes of inspiring others.

Dr. Zhanna Lehmann began her musical education at the Kazan State Musical Conservatory in Russia, earning her Doctorate degree in Choral Conducting at the University of Illinois in 2018. She has been working with choirs in a variety of contexts for over 25 years. She is currently the director for her church choir at St. Nicholas Antiochian Orthodox Church in Urbana. She teaches and does music clinics for the Antiochian Archdiocese at its Sacred Music Institutes. She is also the founder and director of the Illinois Orthodox Choir, a choral group open to singers of all faiths in Champaign-Urbana. The Illinois Orthodox Choir is committed to spreading the beauty of Orthodox music to the general public and has performed in a variety of settings. They have recently released a CD called *Christ, Our Balm in Gilead.* Her chapter, "The Voice of the Heart," is a compelling memoire of how music brought her to, and sustains her in the Orthodox Faith, and the surprising part played by African American Spirituals.

Stratos Mandalakis is a graduate of Fordham University with a BA in Byzantine Studies and Music History/Composition.

He holds an MA in Eastern Christian Theology from the John XXII Institute/Maryknoll School of Theology. He teaches Byzantine Musicology in the Antiochian House of Studies/ Saint Stephen's Course. In Bergenfield, New Jersey, Subdeacon Stratos has been the choir director and head chanter of St. Anthony Antiochian Orthodox Church for the past 20 years. The choir has released a CD entitled *With an Open Heart: Sounds of Worship at St. Anthony Orthodox Church, Bergenfield, N.J.* His tenure with the Spirit of Orthodoxy Choir (SoO) began in 2009. He was named assistant to Founding Artistic Director, Aleksei V. Shipovalnikov, in 2013. Stratos became Artistic Director of SoO in July 2019 and is excited to continue to build and expand upon the work done by the ensemble and his predecessor: to bring people to experience the beauty of Christ's Church as expressed in her glorious music! For this volume, Stratos tells us why he is eager to add Orthodox liturgical music based on the Spirituals to the repertoire of the SoO Choir.

Mikhail Markhasev is working out his salvation as a lifetime prisoner at Corcoran State Prison in California. The late 1980s found him as a confused young immigrant in Southern California. He sought to define his identity by joining an ethnic gang, but this eventually led to his committing murder— the murder of a man of another race. Through the outreach of the Orthodox Christian Prison Ministry, he embraced Christ and is dedicating his life to prayer, study, and service to other inmates. He shares here a powerful testimony about praying the Canon for Racial Reconciliation in prison.

I
SPIRITUALITY

1

FROM THE HEART TO THE HEART
MATUSHKA MICHAILA AND GOSPEL MUSIC

HIEROMONK ALEXII ALTSCHUL

L ET ME TELL YOU ABOUT THELMA, who would become known in Orthodox Christian circles as Matushka* Michaila. Thelma and I were married in 1986. One of the things I will treasure the most about those days was visiting many small black churches with her. There was something so deep and moving when I would hear the deacon begin devotions with "I love the Lord; He heard my cry." Then it was followed by the congregation plaintively repeating the same verse in unison. She would tell me, "That's just how they sang it back home!"

The musical form was referred to as "old meter hymn" in the Baptist tradition. The use of the minor key and the sorrowful, expressive sounds touched a deep place within. I taped an interview in 2012 with Matushka and her sister Roberta, just a few weeks before Matushka passed away. She

---

* Matushka is a Russian term for a priest's wife; it is a diminutive form of "mother."

talked about the similarities between her early life in Texarkana, Arkansas in the Missionary Baptist tradition and her experiences in the Orthodox Church. The practice of baptism by three immersions in the Name of the Father and of the Son and of the Holy Spirit was just one similarity. All night prayer for the departed was another. There were many. But the music that would take a soul from sorrow to joy, from despair to hope was one thing we found in common with Orthodox liturgical texts.

During our first years together, we developed a deep friendship with Rev. Willie Bennett,* Ed Lewis and the Gospel Allstars from Canton, Mississippi. I learned some of these old meter songs and other Gospel songs by heart. I'll never forget the night at Grace's Kitchen, when I was seated at a table with Thelma, her mother Lula, known as "Madea", and her daughter Cherlyn. The Gospel Allstars were performing a concert for the residents of the LaSalle Apartments (attached to Grace's Kitchen). All of a sudden, Reverend announced, "Tonight, we have a special treat. We're gonna have Rev. Dave (me!!) come and join us singing "Just Another Day's Journey." Surprised and a bit embarrassed, I got up. With my quieter, smooth voice I started out, "Just another day's journey and I'm glad..." Then the Allstars belted out the deep, husky refrain, "I'm glad about it!" We made it through the song, and when I sat down, Madea (who was very plain spoken) said to Thelma, "Thelma! Why'd you let that man get up there and make a fool out of hisself?" I started laughing hilariously. I felt the same way! The people sitting in the other tables were kind to me. But I realized something. Although I enjoyed singing it, feeling it, and praying these songs, I had not been through the kind of suffering each of these singers had been through to produce that depth of sound. They used to say, "What's from the heart touches the heart." Most of my approach to singing was from my head first, not my heart.

---

* The Rev. Willie Bennett reposed in 2019.

Yet, Gospel music was always a part of our 26 years of marriage. She loved Sam Cook and the Soul Stirrers, the Jackson Southernaires, the Mighty Clouds of Joy, and many more. Both her mother (Madea) and her father, George, were Gospel singers for a period in Arkansas and Louisiana. When her soul would feel down, she'd put on some Gospel music, start "pattin'" her hands, and soon her soul would be lifted up. The very last Sunday of her life, March 11, 2012, she woke up and wanted to sing Gospel songs together. We listened and sang for hours with tears of joy and thankfulness. Two days later she reposed.

Shortly after we became Orthodox Christians in 1993, my godfather, Bishop Gerasim* (at the time a simple monk from St. Herman of Alaska Monastery in Platina, California) encouraged Michaila and me to contact people to have a conference on the relationship between Ancient Christianity and African Americans. In addition, one of the monks, Fr. Damascene Christensen (now abbot) had been studying about the spiritual significance of the Spirituals and suffering Christianity. So, in February 1994, we had our first of what is now 29 conferences this year. (The text of his talk is published in the first volume of the Unbroken Circle Series, *Foundations: 1994–1997,* which is a compilation of several talks from the first few conferences.)

After hearing Fr. Damascene talk about the Spirituals, we spontaneously started singing the old Spiritual "Wade in the Water" during the Baptism service that following Lazarus Saturday, 1994. It stuck. For the next twenty years, when we would perform Baptisms at St. Mary of Egypt Orthodox Church in Kansas City, Missouri, that became part of the service. While the newly baptized went to change their clothes and were preparing for their white baptismal robe, we would sing,

---

* Presently, the Right Reverend Gerasim, Bishop of Fort Worth, Auxiliary to the Diocese of the South, Orthodox Church in America.

Wade in the water!
Wade in the water, children,
Wade in the water.
God's gonna trouble the water.
    See those children dressed in white?
God's gonna trouble the water.
    Looks to me like an Israelite.
God's gonna trouble the water.
Wade in the water!
Wade in the water, children,
Wade in the water.
God's gonna trouble the water.

Within the Orthodox tradition, symbols and icons are an integral part of our faith. In Greek, *symbolos* (symbol) conveys the idea of gathering together, whereas *diabolos* (devil, diabolic) conveys scattering, breaking apart. Symbols and icons and people are blessed with holy water. They do not merely stand for a deeper meaning. They themselves are carriers and transmitters of divine grace after the blessing. They draw us into communion and unity. There is a thin veil between the sanctified matter and the spiritual reality. This is why the Ark of the Covenant was venerated. Why the Cross is venerated. Why the Gospels are venerated. Why bread and wine become the Body and Blood of Christ. Why water becomes holy water. *The material has been made holy.* This is why it is customary for us to honor the human body with prayerful burial. It is the "temple of the Holy Spirit" (1 Cor 6:19).

Music is like this. There are deeper meanings. During slavery, when "Wade in the Water" was sung at baptisms, it was reminding slaves of their spiritual deliverance provided through Christ. It was an echo from Egypt, when the Hebrew slaves were set free from bondage to Pharaoh in the Red Sea by following Moses. For the early Christians, the same theme was applied to our being set free from the slavery of sin and the devil through the waters of Baptism to now follow Christ (cf. 1 Cor 10:1–4).

In the divine services of the Orthodox Church, these themes are repeated in many services. When we celebrate Matins (a morning prayer service), the first *ode** typically begins with a reference to the deliverance from Egypt. Here is an example from a service to the Lord Jesus Christ:

> In the deep of old the infinite Power overwhelmed Pharaoh's whole army. But the incarnate Word annihilated pernicious sin. Exceedingly glorious is the Lord, for gloriously is He glorified.†

During the Great Blessing of the Water, and during the Baptism service, there are many readings and prayers referring to the deliverance from Egypt and its spiritual significance. Here are two prayers from that service for the Blessing of Water:

> That Satan may be swiftly crushed beneath our feet, and that every counsel that is directed against us by the Evil One may be made of no effect, let us pray to the Lord.

> *Lord have mercy*

> That He will deliver us from every attack and temptation of the Adversary and make us worthy of the good things that are promised, let us pray to the Lord.

> *Lord have mercy*‡

An archpriest in the Orthodox Church, Fr. Michael Carney, said:

---

* Ode: In Orthodox Christian services, an ode (canticle) is based on one of nine songs from Biblical stories that comprise what is known as a canon, a structured hymn. Some of the stories are the deliverance from Egypt, Jonah delivered from the whale, the three Hebrew young men delivered from the fire, and the song of the Mother of God in finding out she was to give birth to the Messiah.

† Ode One Irmos of the Canon to our Lord Jesus Christ. An "irmos" is the first stanza of the "ode" of a canon (see note above).

‡ From the Litany during the Great Blessing of the Waters. A "litany" is a sequence of prayers for mercy during Orthodox Christian services.

The Grace of the compassionate God met the suffering and faith of the slaves, and produced these rich hymns. We can sense a real meeting here, what the Orthodox call a "synergy"—a working together of the God who saves and the people who need and want salvation so deep they can taste it. God taught the slaves to see their own story in the story of Moses and the Israelites, and every human story in light of Christ. The same insight is expressed in a different kind of poetry in hymns like this:[1]

> Of old Thou didst bury the pursuing tyrant
> Beneath the waves of the sea;
> Now the children of those who were saved
> Bury Thee beneath the earth.
> But like the children, let us sing to the Lord
> For He has been greatly glorified.*[2]

It was that rich interweaving of symbolism between African American spiritual expression and Orthodox hymnography that led us to sing a Spiritual during the Baptismal services. But that awareness did not begin with me. I'll never forget attending the first Orthodox Divine Liturgy with my wife, Thelma (Michaila), at Holy Trinity Orthodox Church, at that time in downtown Kansas City, Kansas. I was a Protestant pastor seriously considering Orthodoxy. Thelma was concerned that I would get confused with all my reading. She reluctantly agreed to go.

As I was "watching" the movement of the Liturgy, listening to the chanting, and trying to figure out the comparisons between Orthodoxy and Evangelical Christianity, I felt her poke me in the ribs. She looked at me with such an inspired look, and said, "I'm in heaven! I don't know about you, but I'm becoming Orthodox!!!" She explained that these weren't just pictures of Michael and Gabriel the Archangels. The angels were there!

---

* The hymn is from the Matins canon for Holy Saturday in tone 6: Irmos, Ode 1.

Again, as I was approaching it from my head, she immediately intuited it from her heart! She embraced the ancient Orthodox Church and never looked back. For her, the connecting with the saints in the services of the Orthodox Church, the connecting with the woman at the well (St. Photini) in the song "Jesus Gave Me Water" by Sam Cook, the connecting with her righteous Cherokee great-grandmother, Miss Mayella (the "closest thing I knew to a saint," as she said), were all part of this invisible reality of the Holy Orthodox Church. Since they were in heaven with Christ they are in the Orthodox Church! This unity of the Faith went all the way back to her time when she was a child in Texarkana, Arkansas under Jim Crow. Some people from a white church told her, "Don't worry dear. In heaven there will be a black heaven, and a white heaven, so all will be okay." She immediately felt, "NO! There's just one Jesus! One heaven!"

For Matushka, it was the same with music. When she would chant "O Gentle Light" in Vespers, or "It is Truly Meet" to the Mother of God or the Thomas Dorsey hymn, "Precious Lord," or "Walk with Me Lord," she knew it was the same Jesus. It was the same Holy Trinity. It was the same Lord. It was the same Virgin Mary. Somehow, she knew that the bishops and theologians would figure out a way to describe it and bring it all together. But the underlying reality is that there is *one* heaven and *one* God in three Persons, Father, Son, and Holy Spirit.

2

SINGING THE LORD'S SONG

THE THEOLOGY OF AMERICAN SLAVE SPIRITUALS

FR. DEACON JONATHAN REAVIS

I F YOU WANT TO KNOW what a church believes, listen to its songs. For the Orthodox Church, theology is profoundly manifest in the poetic and beautiful hymns sung in the Divine Liturgy and in the daily offices. In the case of American slave Spirituals, however, the matter of what enslaved black Christians believed is a bit more ambiguous. The ubiquity of these Spirituals among the wider American worshipping communities has presented some interpretive challenges. The hymns of the Orthodox Church live almost exclusively with communities of Orthodox believers. By contrast, the Spirituals have spread well beyond the confines of the American slave community and have been adopted by Christian communities with no real connection to the lived experience of America's enslaved Christians. Indeed, the Spirituals have been, as the Psalmist says, "the Lord's song in a strange land" (Ps 137:4). Therefore, identifying the unique theology of the American slave Spirituals requires examining them within their context and allowing the experiences of the enslaved community to inform how these hymns are read.

In this chapter, I will use the testimony of enslaved African Americans to analyze the theological content of several popular Spirituals. I will examine ways that these Spirituals have been misinterpreted, how they might be more faithfully understood, and how their theological content relates to that of the ancient Christian tradition. Since I come from an Orthodox perspective my theological analysis will reflect that. However, as a Korean American, I do not have the hermeneutic advantage of being connected in any real way to the African American religious tradition. That said, I will do my best to utilize the sources available to me to both elevate black perspectives on these Spirituals and to highlight what I believe are profound theological insights.

Misinterpretations

LIKE MANY AMERICAN PROTESTANTS, I spent much of my religious upbringing unaware that I sang African American slave Spirituals on many a Sunday morning. My family hopped between a handful of Protestant denominations during my childhood, but several Spirituals were sung throughout. Some of these songs had a profound impact on me and were quite formative for my spiritual consciousness. To this day, the words of "Lord, I Want to Be a Christian" form a sung prayer on my lips when I find myself struggling with faith. It wasn't until I was a young adult that I realized that I had been edified and encouraged for years by the singing tradition of black Christians that had been enslaved in this country. By the same token, I had become overly critical of some of the theology contained within these Spirituals, due in large part to my ignorance of the context in which they were written. In my twenties, when I started to critically examine the Protestant faith I had inherited in my childhood, I erroneously decided that songs like "Swing Low, Sweet Chariot" were too escapist, assuming they emphasized an otherworldly focus

11

and abandonment of a suffering world. I failed to realize this song's relationship to a suffering slave community. So, not only did the Spirituals anonymously influence my spiritual life, but my ignorance of their origins also influenced my interpretation of their theology.

The Spirituals have suffered this sort of interpretive violence for nearly their entire history. They were composed by and for black Christians suffering under American slavery. Once America abolished institutional slavery, however, the popularity of the Spirituals grew both in white congregations and as elements of popular culture. Eventually, the Spirituals became an object of inquiry for academics seeking to understand the history and legacy of American slavery. White interest in the Spiritual was likely stimulated by the work of former slave, abolitionist, and AME Zion Methodist Minister, Frederick Douglass. In his autobiography, Douglass argued that every "sorrow song" he heard as a child was in fact "a testimony against slavery, and a prayer to God for deliverance from chains."[*1] As the popularity of the Spirituals grew, this testimony against slavery and the prayer for deliverance became obscured. The Spirituals continued to be sung in historic black churches in America, but for the majority of white Americans, much was lost in their transmission. Writing in the early twentieth century, W. E. B. Du Bois suggested that the soul of the Spirituals had been missed by white audiences:

> The mass of "gospel" hymns which has swept through American churches and well-nigh ruined our sense of song consists largely of debased imitations of Negro melodies made by ears that caught the jingle but not the music, the body but not the soul, of the Jubilee songs.[2]

---

* *Editor's note:* For further understanding of how the Spirituals became an object of inquiry for academics, see Nun Katherine Weston's chapter in this volume: "A Brief History of Spirituals and Gospel Music," p. 131.

For Du Bois, a connection to the life and experiences of the community of slaves was crucial to not only the proper understanding of the Spirituals, but also the proper use of them. In his time, the Spirituals had gained popularity based on aesthetic merit, but Du Bois recognized that the true significance of these hymns required an understanding of their history and their community of origin. Echoing Du Bois, theologian James Cone identified the deep need for a religious understanding of the Spirituals:

> To interpret the religious significance of that spiritual for the black community, "academic" tools are not enough. The interpreter must feel the Spirit; that is, one must feel one's way into the power of black music, responding both to its rhythm and the faith in experience it affirms.[3]

It is with this understanding that I attempt to discover the religious significance of the Spiritual and its theology.

Carry Me Home:
Earthly *and* Heavenly Freedom

IT IS ONLY through the eyes of a suffering slave community that the Spirituals can be properly understood. The popular hymn, "Swing Low, Sweet Chariot" illustrates the divergence between the interpretation within the community of origin and that from without:

> Swing low, sweet chariot,
> Coming for to carry me home,
> Swing low, sweet chariot,
> Coming for to carry me home.
> I looked over Jordan and what did I see
> Coming for to carry me home?
> A band of angels coming after me
> Coming for to carry me home.[4]

Having been raised in a Protestant, dispensationalist tradition, my reading of this hymn used to conjure images of the rapture, the moment God comes to "carry home" the faithful, rescuing them from a world destined for destruction. According to this interpretation, "home" was the eventual heavenly destination of the saved and "Jordan" became little more than momentary earthly discomfort or even bodily existence itself. My understanding of the rapture implied that Christians shouldn't be expected to suffer at all, and I sang this song as a prayer to be spared any potential tribulation. In my twenties, I grew a distaste for this type of theology, largely because in my context—which was mostly comfortable and lacked any real suffering—any notions of deliverance from this world were associated with an unhealthy escapism. This reading of "Swing Low" was not a prayer to be delivered from a current experience of suffering, but a hope that I might pass from this life into the next with relatively little discomfort. This is obviously not what Wallace Willis, a former slave and the composer of "Swing Low," had in mind when he wrote this hymn.[5]

Wallace Willis was a slave in Oklahoma and labored near the Red River, a possible inspiration for the line about the biblical River Jordan. When Willis wrote this hymn, he was drawing on his experiences and merged them with biblical stories. When Willis says he "looked over Jordan," his use of poetic language was not conjuring imaginary scenarios. Unlike my experience of the song, which involved me abstracting the language of the Bible to form a rough spiritual metaphor for my life, Willis drew from his direct experience of longing to cross a literal river and experience both spiritual and physical liberation. The Spirituals, therefore, contained multiple meanings often obscured from the non-slave. One meaning of this hymn spoke directly to the hope of literal freedom from slavery.

In "Swing Low," "home" could be interpreted as heaven, but it could also represent "the North" as the physical location of freedom for slaves in the 19th century. In the biblical story of Exodus, Jordan was the last river to cross before entering the land of Canaan, the promised home of the Israelites. It is not hard to imagine Wallace Willis looking over the Red River in

Oklahoma and thinking about a land of freedom from slavery, perhaps recalling Joshua crossing the Jordan into Canaan. Enslaved African Americans often identified with the sojourning people of Israel, and so in this context, Jordan represented both death as the passage over into paradise *and* the journey North as the final barrier to "Canaan Land."

Frederick Douglass, writing on his experience of the religious practices of the slave community in the early 19th century, disclosed the dual meaning of what he called the slave "sorrow songs." He wrote, "A keen observer might have detected in our repeated singing of 'O Canaan, sweet Canaan, I am bound for the land of Canaan,' something more than a hope of reaching heaven. We meant to reach the north—and the north was our Canaan."[6] Further on, recalling his plans to escape his master's plantation, Douglass referred to slavery as his "Egypt." Another Spiritual originating in the Northern Seaboard states like Maryland, where Douglass was born, also made use of the Canaan motif. The song's refrain echoed the affirmation, "Canaan is the land for me," followed by the plea, "Let God's saints come in," the hymn's title.[7] In the Spirituals, Canaan represents both the heavenly home and the state of freedom from slavery. For white slaveholders, the former interpretation was perhaps the most obvious and least problematic. The latter meaning, however, was largely obscured from their understanding.

Indeed, in the minds of slaveholders not only was Christianity not problematic to the position of "owning" slaves, but it was also at times construed as condoning it. Citing such biblical passages as St. Paul's admonition to slaves to be obedient to their masters in Ephesians, slave masters thought Christianity useful for producing docile and obedient slaves. Often, slaveholders assumed the role of spiritual leader over their plantation, which made the curation of a slavery-friendly version of Christianity possible.[8] However, the faith of the Bible—that is, the faith that bore witness to the Liberator of the slaves of Egypt and the faith that proclaimed freedom for the captives—often had the opposite of the slaveholders' intended effect. Contrary to the instruction of slave masters, pro-slavery catechists, and clergy, the enslaved believed baptism into the Christian faith imparted equal status with their masters in the eyes of God, and their songs reflected this conviction.[9] Another song by Wallace Willis, "Steal Away to Jesus," illustrates the "subversive" nature of the faith of the American slaves.

I Ain't Got Long To Stay Here: Seeking Deliverance

THE ROLE that "Steal Away" played in calling enslaved Christians to clandestine religious meetings is well documented in many slave narratives. Subverting the pro-slavery version of the Christianity of their masters, the enslaved began meeting in secret to pray to Christ the Liberator. These secret religious gatherings often took place in the cover of darkness, in camps or cabins away from the sight of slaveholders.

"Steal Away" was sung as a sort of signal that the secret prayer meeting was about to begin. Frederick Douglass made mention of a variation on the hymn: "'Run to Jesus—shun the danger—I don't expect to stay Much longer here,' was a favorite air, and had a double meaning." He expounded on the dual meaning of stealing away, saying,

> In the lips of some, it meant the expectation of a speedy summons to a world of spirits; but, in the lips of our company, it simply meant, a speedy pilgrimage toward a free state, and deliverance from all the evils and dangers of slavery.[10]

For Douglass, "stealing away to Jesus" involved both the retreat to a spiritual gathering and the hope for a deliverance from slavery in this world.

Perhaps the most noteworthy example of the use of this hymn for subverting slavery is the slave revolt of Nat Turner in 1831. After escaping slavery as a young man in 1825, Turner returned, believing that he was called by God to liberate others from slavery. According to his testimony at his trial, Turner experienced divine visions, featuring imagery reminiscent of the biblical Apocalypse. He saw "white spirits and black spirits engaged in battle, and the sun was darkened— the thunder rolled in the Heavens, and blood flowed in streams."[11] Turner also heard a voice directing him to enact this heavenly battle. Turner believed that God was leading and directing his efforts toward freedom, and that "the great day of judgment was at hand."[12] According to some accounts, Turner recruited enslaved warriors to his cause using the song "Steal Away to Jesus," which itself contains apocalyptic imagery. The second verse contains the following lines:

> My Lord, He calls me,
> He calls me by the thunder,
> The trumpet sounds within-a my soul,
> I ain't got long to stay here.[13]

For Turner and those that joined him, these words were not merely symbolic, and their application was not confined to the afterlife. God was being imminently revealed as the Liberator of the enslaved. Turner and his followers attempted to free Virginian slaves by force over the course of a few days. The revolt was quickly quelled, and Turner evaded authorities for several months, but he was eventually captured. He was tried for "conspiring to rebel and making insurrection," was found guilty, and was executed. Turner's actions had far-reaching effects and brought to light the fact that many of the enslaved awaited an imminent liberation from their chains. No longer could slaveholders assume that the freedom that their slaves prayed for was merely symbolic or "spiritual." The freedom of the Spirituals had real-world implications.

In the aftermath of Turner's rebellion, slaveholders cracked down on slave-led religious meetings. Charity Bowery, a former slave, remembered that there were attempts to quell any residual sentiments toward revolt in the wake of Nat Turner's apocalyptic actions. She said, "All the colored folks were afraid to pray in the time of the old Prophet Nat." She also recalled that slaveholders and militant whites became far more suspicious of the recitation of slave songs and that some "whites would fall upon any slaves they heard praying, or singing a hymn, and often killed them."[14] Charity recited a song that was prohibited after Turner's rebellion, saying, "They thought we was going to rise, because we sung 'better days are coming.'"[15] One of the verses from that song read:

> Some friends has gone before me,
> I must try to go and meet them,
> Glory, Hallelujah![16]

Prior to Turner's insurrectionary movement, these words might have registered to slaveholders as poetic language articulating the hope of a heavenly reunion with loved ones. Now, in the wake of a militant slave rebellion, these words took on new meaning. Perhaps the slaves were singing about joining friends that had escaped slavery by going north. What is more, the songs petitioned God for that freedom, which indicated that enslaved Christians thought of God as sympathetic to their plight. In response, many slaveholders in the South prohibited their slaves from holding self-directed religious meetings. Nevertheless, many slave communities continued to meet in secret. One former slave from Arkansas, Lucretia Alexander, recalled her small community singing hymns and praying with hushed voices once or twice a week.[17] Another former slave from South Carolina named Fannie Moore recalled how her so-called slave master prohibited education and church, knowing that they made slaves "harder to manage," but that the enslaved still stole off and held their own prayer meetings.[18] One former slave recalled that slave preachers were expected to preach obedience to their masters, but that in the secret meetings, they would "pray for better things."[19] The Spirituals were at once a cry to God to correct the injustice of slavery and the encouragement for slaves to pursue their freedom.

It has become something of a trend in contemporary study of the Spirituals to impose a purely materialist reading of these songs, stripping them of all religious meaning. Assuming the Spirituals were a *merely* symbolic medium for conveying politically subversive or abolitionist ideas requires the dismissal of genuinely held religious belief. Any careful reading of slave narratives will contradict this notion. It was not the case that the Spirituals were merely coded propaganda used by slaves who "knew better" than to actually believe in their spiritual meanings. On the contrary, slave martyrs such as Ezekiel and Martin gave their lives, not in the course of rebellion, but because they continued to gather in prayer despite violent attempts to quell their religious fervor.[20] The prayer meetings and the recitation of the Spirituals meant more than how they might serve the cause of liberation from slavery. The revolutionary spirit of Nat Turner never gained widespread momentum, and so it must be the case that the Spirituals served more than to simply fan the flames of rebellion. The theological legacy of the Spirituals ultimately derives not from their ability to resist enslavement, but from their ability to transform the experience of it—an aspect of the Spirituals that I will return to later.

Perhaps the most profound theological insight that can be gleaned from the abolitionist content in the Spirituals is the idea that God is actively involved in the world. Setting aside the complicated discussion of the morality of Turner's rebellion, his actions and their reception by the community of slaves reveal a belief in a God that cares for the suffering. Far from the Spirituals' articulating empty prayers that only serve as vehicles for revolutionary content, we find instead hymns that express a deep faith and trust in a God who intervenes. The enslaved Christians really believed that God heard their sorrow songs and expected Him to answer. It should come as no surprise, then, that the slaves identified deeply with the Exodus story.

Howard Thurman, 20th century theologian and descendent of enslaved African Americans, observed that slaves resonated with Israel as "children of destiny."[21] While reading the Old Testament, the composers of the Spirituals drew on their experience of enslavement, which they shared with the Israelites, and chiefly understood their God as Liberator. Importantly, this meant that God was involved in human history. As Thurman puts it, "He manifested himself in certain specific acts that seemed to be over and above the historic process itself."[22] Interestingly, the belief in God's character as Deliverer was not limited to a specific people, race, or ethnic group. By identifying so thoroughly with the Israelites, enslaved blacks transcended the racial categories that were used by whites to justify their enslavement. The fact that enslaved American Christians could see themselves in the Exodus story speaks not only to their conviction that God liberates, but that He does so for all oppressed people. According to the Spirituals, the God of the Old Testament was not one that was "a respecter of persons," swayed or influenced by prejudices or racial preference. The fact that God liberated slaves from Egypt necessarily meant that He could—and would—liberate slaves from the oppression of American chattel slavery. Inversely, the belief in God's ability to intervene in their plight also meant that enslaved American Christians believed that the Exodus story relayed true events. As Thurman says, "They were literalists in their interpretations, not only because such was the dominant pattern of the religious thinking of the environment, but also because their needs demanded it."[23] The Spirituals were not merely poetic articulations of general concepts about God. They were testimonies of faith in the God who saves.

Regarding the expectation of God's intervention in world events, there are parallels to the Orthodox tradition. The story of the origins of the Akathist* to the Mother of God seems the most applicable here, as it involves an Orthodox hymn. In summary, during the seventh century, Constantinople was under siege and militarily outnumbered—hopelessly so—by

---

* Akathist: a hymn containing 12 sections with refrains, usually in praise of the Lord, His Mother, saints or angels.

the invading Persian and Avar armies. In response, Patriarch Sergius made daily processions around the city walls with the icon of the Mother of God. Suffering great losses, it seemed as if Constantinople would fall, but miraculously, the Byzantine navy turned the enemy fleet back from the sea. Accompanying this final stand, the enemy forces were confronted by an appearance of the Theotokos.[24] The Akathist to the Mother of God was sung in thanksgiving for victory during the attack. The ancient text of the Akathist forms the basis for the Kontakion to the Theotokos:

> To thee, the Champion Leader, we thy servants dedicate a feast of victory and of thanksgiving as ones rescued out of sufferings, O Theotokos; but as thou art one with might which is invincible, from all dangers that can be do thou deliver us, that we may cry to thee: Rejoice, thou Bride unwedded.[25]

This hymn not only expresses belief in God's power through the Theotokos based on past events, it also asks for continued protection and deliverance from danger. As in the Spirituals, the petition for protection is not abstract or only symbolic. In the hymns of the Church, there is a belief in God's power to deliver from physical dangers, as well as spiritual ones. This belief in God's involvement in world events is a feature of both Orthodox hymns and the African American Spirituals.

The Trumpet Sounds Within My Soul:
Imminent Spiritual Liberation

FOR ENSLAVED CHRISTIANS, the hope of salvation concerned both body and soul. Naturally, freedom was a frequent theme in their Spirituals, yet often articulated in a way that was not dependent upon earthly conditions. The dual meaning of freedom in the Spirituals referred to the freedom of the body in emancipation from slavery *and* the freedom of the soul in paradise. However, both freedoms were equally remote for this community—neither the liberty of heaven nor the North was immediately available. As a result, the Spirituals articulat-ed a *spiritual* freedom, a condition of the soul in the here-and-now that transcended physical and temporal limitations. Returning to "Steal Away to Jesus," we see that the hymn not only related to the efforts to escape bodily enslavement, it also expressed a deep struggle for the liberation of the soul.

> Steal away, steal away, steal away to Jesus!
> Steal away, steal away home
> I ain't got long to stay here.

> My Lord, He calls me,
> He calls me by the thunder,
> The trumpet sounds within-a my soul,
> I ain't got long to stay here.

> Green trees a-bending, po' sinner stand a-trembling,
> The trumpet sounds within-a my soul,
> I ain't got long to stay here,
> Oh, Lord I ain't got long to stay here.[26]

This hymn contains at least three interpretations. A historical/literal interpretation has already been discussed, which relates to the hope for freedom from slavery. The hymn very obviously also draws on apocalyptic imagery, which resonated deeply with Nat Turner. Language relating to the sounding of the trumpets and the thunder can be interpreted within an eschatological framework, relaying the hope for Christ's eventual return and restoration of all things in the age to come. The "green trees a-bending" may be a reference to Ezekiel 17:24, an apocalyptic passage that reads:

> And all the trees of the field shall know that I, the Lord, have brought down the high tree and exalted the low tree, dried up the green tree and made the dry tree flourish; I, the Lord, have spoken and have done it.

According to this Spiritual, injustices will be corrected in the age to come, and those with health and power will be hum-bled. These uses of the Apocalypse, however, do not exhaust the meaning of this hymn. Thomas Talley, chemist, African

American folk song commentator, and child of former slaves, illumined another hidden meaning of "Steal Away":

> To the listening master it meant that the Negro was think-
> ing of what a short time it would be before he would die
> and leave the earth, but to the listening slaves it meant that
> he was thinking of how short a time it would be before he
> left the cotton field for a pleasant religious meeting.[27]

Contained within this Spiritual is a deeply personal application of the Apocalypse. On the one hand, the song antici-
pates a personal exit from this world—distinct from the cos-
mic judgement of the world that slaveholders assumed was
being invoked. The personal nature of the song is quite evident by the use of the first-person singular. On the other
hand, Talley seems to apply a more imminent interpretation
that need not involve death, the Second Coming of Christ, or
a literal deliverance from slavery. "Steal Away" spoke not only
to those forms of liberation, but also to a kind of freedom
found in assembling for prayer and worship. In this interpretation, the meeting itself, and the recitation of the sorrow
songs, provided access to a mystical "land of freedom." This
interpretation is further supported by the song, "Deep River":

> Deep river, my home is over Jordan,
> Deep river, Lord,
> I want to cross over into campground.
>
> Oh chillun,
> Oh, don't you want to go, to that gospel feast,
> That promised land, that land, where all is peace?
> Walk into heaven, and take my seat,
> And cast my crown at Jesus feet.[28]

Although not directly mentioned, the Canaan motif is again
presented in this hymn as "over Jordan" and "that promised
land." As with "Swing Low" and "Steal Away," a plurality of
meanings may be identified. The song draws on the Exodus
story, with the singer identifying with the sojourning people of
God. An element not captured in text is the musicality of these

songs. The slow pace of "Deep River" accentuates the laborious journey described by the words, and the longing to find rest in the land "where all is peace." The song embodies a weariness with the world of suffering, and yet preserves a hope for rest. That rest may be interpreted as the literal ending of slavery, but it also may mean the end of suffering in death or the eschaton. Lastly, however, is the meaning mentioned in "Steal Away": the rest found in the secret prayer meetings, here signified by the mention of "campground." During the Great Awakening of the 18th century, touring camp revival meetings attracted many converts to Christianity, including the enslaved.[29] The mention of "campground" in this song may indicate the ecstatic experience of prayer in revival gatherings and in the secret prayer meetings of enslaved Christians. "Campground," then, is not only connected to heaven, but also to prayer and worship. The mention of "gospel feast" also lends itself to the idea that the slave prayer gatherings participated in heavenly realities. Another Spiritual called "There's a Great Camp Meeting" makes the link between heaven and the prayer gatherings explicit with the words, "There's a great camp meeting in the Promise Land."[30]

Through the secret meetings, the enslaved had contact with paradise, not merely in a metaphorical sense, but in true spiritual communion with God. For the singers of these Spirituals, the gathering for prayer and worship did not just provide psychological comfort to their suffering. The gatherings also provided spiritual comfort and access to the land "beyond Jordan" —the much longed for heavenly home. Spiritual freedom was not confined to the afterlife or to the North. The chain of slavery was broken by the praise of God. The liberty of heaven broke into the world of the slave, spilling out from eternity into the night gatherings of enslaved worshipers.

The theological insight gleaned from this interpretation is that slaves did not believe the spiritual realm was impenetrable. They accessed heaven through gathering together for prayer. As Christ says in the Gospel, "For where two or three are gathered together in My name, I am there in the midst of them" (Mt 18:20). This belief goes back to the very foundations of the Christian faith. In Orthodox Tradition, the idea that worship is mystically linked to the heavenly realm is explicit within the Liturgy of St. John Chrysostom. The Cherubic Hymn is just one example of this in the hymnography:

> Let us who mystically represent the Cherubim, and chant the thrice-holy hymn unto the life-creating Trinity, now lay aside all earthly care.

Here, "represent" should not be understood as signifying something that is absent, but rather imaging and participating in something real and spiritually manifest. In Orthodox worship, the faithful are transported into heaven, and the mysteries of eternity are made present. Likewise, for enslaved singers of the Spirituals, heaven was not located "somewhere else," completely cut off from this world. Rather, they believed, as Christ said, "the kingdom of God is within you" (Lk 17:21). So we see that the theology of the Spirituals transcended geography and blended the earthly with the heavenly. Closely related to the belief in heaven's proximity is the accessibility of biblical characters and saints. Just as the Cherubic Hymn suggests that participation in heavenly realities means proximity to the angels, so too do the Spirituals articulate a kind of belief in the present communion with the saints in heaven.

Hold Your Light, Sister Mary:
Communion of the Saints

THE HYMN, "Hold Your Light" not only employs the image of a promised land of freedom, it also contains a dialogue with biblical characters:

> What make ole Satan to follow me so?
> Satan hain't nottin' at all for to do wid me. (Run seeker.)
> Hold your light, (Sister Mary,)

Hold your light, (Seeker turn back,)
Hold your light on Canaan shore.[31]

As with the other Spirituals discussed, both historical and theological interpretations may be applied. From the historical perspective, Satan might be understood to represent an overseer or "patroller" on the hunt for an escaped slave. In this hymn, the Seeker—Satan or the overseer—is repeatedly told to turn back and abandon his pursuit of the liberated fugitive. Satan can also be understood literally as the supernatural enemy of God and His people. In this case, Satan attempts to prevent the pilgrim from entering Canaan, or heaven.

The hymn also implores the assistance of "Sister Mary." Many slave Spirituals reference both Mary Magdalene and Mary the Mother of Jesus. Here we see the hymn's fluid chronology—Mary being a New Testament character, while Canaan was the promised land to the Old Testament nation of Israel. As to which Mary is referenced here, Mary Magdalene or Mary the Mother of God, the question might be answered by examining another hymn, "Run, Mary, Run," which begins with the lines:

Run, Mary, run
Run, Mary, run
Oh, run, Mary, run,
I know de udder worl' is not like dis.
Oh, not like dis.[32]

The Mary referenced in this Spiritual is most likely Mary Magdalene, who, in the Gospel of John, was the first to encounter the Risen Christ in the Garden of Gethsemane and was subsequently told to bring news of the Resurrection to the other disciples. This hymn joins Christ in encouraging Mary to run with the Gospel news. Here, we see yet another dimension of the blended chronology and biblical images in the Spirituals. The other world referenced is both heaven and the new world of the Resurrection. By linking the story of Mary Magdalene with the "other world," this hymn again affirms the belief in heaven's proximity, effected by Christ's Resurrection. The glory of the Resurrection is therefore neither confined to the past nor reserved only for the future, but is dynamically present. Likewise, the biblical character of Mary is also not only in the past, or even dwelling beyond an impenetrable veil in the world to come. Mary continues her initial ministry as the Apostle to the Apostles (as Orthodox tradition puts it) in the present. In this hymn, she bears news of the other world, which unlike this one, is not marked by suffering and death. Likewise, "Hold Your Light" beckons Sister Mary to hold the light of Canaan—the world of the Resurrection—as the singer seeks to flee the pursuit of Satan and death. Mary Magdalene continues to bear the light of the Gospel, holding out hope for all who seek refuge from a harsh world.

The second verse of "Run, Mary, Run" makes mention of Jordan as "a river to cross," and, continuing the Exodus imagery, implores the actions of Moses and Joshua, saying, "Stretch yo' rod an' come across."[33] Here, as with "Hold Your Light," the New Testament character of Mary Magdalene is joined to Moses and Joshua and the narrative of Israel's liberation. By combining these biblical images, this Spiritual identifies the Exodus story with Christ's Resurrection, not unlike the Orthodox tradition of associating Pascha with the feast of Passover.*

The remaining verses of "Run, Mary, Run" contain a familiar refrain: "Swing low, sweet chariot," anticipating passage into the other world, asking to "Let God's children have some peace." The final verse makes explicit mention of Judgement

---

* Western Christianity tends to associate Christ's sacrifice with the Jewish Day of Atonement, often placing emphasis on removing the guilt of sin. While this association is present in the Orthodox liturgical tradition—most notably in the prayer the priest recites after administering communion, which quotes Isaiah 6:7—Orthodox hymnography about the Passion more often evokes Passover. This is most obvious in the hymns for Pascha itself, which focus on Christ's liberation of humanity from the dominion of Satan, sin, and death.

Day, and that "Ev'ry sinner would want to pray" in preparation.[34] Spirituals that make mention of the Day of Judgement apply the image on both a personal and collective scale. A hymn titled "The Day of Judgment" articulated a longing for God's final and eternal deliverance of justice. The song promises God's sheep a place at His right hand, "But de goats must go to de left."[35] When read alongside another hymn, "Lis'en to de Lams," it is evident that the lambs "all a-cryin'" are meant to represent the suffering slave community.[36] Another Spiritual refers directly to the biblical vision of St. John: "Yes, the Book of Revelations will be brought forth dat day, An' ev'ry leaf unfolded, the book of the seven seals." A later line envisions the binding of Satan, effectively imposing the chains of slavery upon God's enemy: "An' den I see ole Satan, an' dey bound him wid a chain." In contrast, the saved are seen "standing on God's right hand."[37] Here, the apocalyptic imagery served to encourage enslaved Christians that their suffering did not go unnoticed, and that their enslavement would be reversed, and that the oppressor would be oppressed. These explicitly eschatological hymns envisioned a future where the injustices of the wicked are corrected. Although these hymns emphasize God's *future* saving action, the eschatological dimension proclaimed God's *eternal* condemnation of slavery. These apocalyptic slave songs insisted that suffering was temporary and that God was opposed to institutions that perpetuated wickedness.

The Spirituals about the Final Judgement also portrayed an understanding of the relationship between conduct on earth and the eternal consequences related to that conduct. It was not simply a given that anyone who professed belief in Christ would necessarily enjoy the eternal salvation He promised to His followers. As one Spiritual says, "But everybody talking 'bout Heaven, Ain't going there."[38] This truth was especially potent for the slaves that suffered under masters who considered themselves to be Christians. For the original singers of these Spirituals, the eschaton was necessarily connected to the temporal life, which involved preparation and repentance. The same God that was involved with history was also involved in the soul of each believer. The heavenly realm, which was immediately accessible through prayer, only admitted suffering lambs into eternity. And just as identification with Mary Magdalene brought slaves close to the site of the Resurrection, so too would identification with the Suffering Lamb bring slaves into paradise.

The slaves' identification with Jesus in the Spirituals is firstly rooted in the theological conviction that Jesus identified with the slaves. The Spirituals bear witness to a deep understanding of Christ's solidarity with the poor, the marginalized, and the oppressed. As Howard Thurman has astutely observed,

> For if Jesus, who is Saviour, is King, then the humble lot of the worshiper is illumined and lifted. The human spirit makes a dual demand with reference to God—that God be vast, the Lord of Life, Creator, Ruler, King, in a sense imperial; and that He also be intimate, primary, personal.[39]

The belief in Jesus' divine and human natures impacted how the Spirituals interpreted the God of the Old Testament.

Way Down in Egypt Land:
Jesus in Both Testaments

A SUBTLE MANIFESTATION of Marcionism exists in the minds of many contemporary Christians, positing some conflict between the God depicted in the Old Testament and the person of Jesus Christ. In this paradigm, the God in the Old Testament is thought to be concerned with "the law" and punishment, while Jesus is conceived as merciful and loving. This duality is mostly foreign to the theology of the slave Spirituals, which, as we have seen, combine the stories of the New and Old Testaments. Importantly, the God who delivered the Israelites from slavery in Egypt is understood to be the same God as Jesus Christ. The song "Come Down" demonstrates this belief:

Come down
Come down, my Lord,
Come down
    Way down in Egypt land.

Jesus Christ, He died for me
    Way down in Egypt land,
Jesus Christ, He set me free
    Way down in Egypt land.

Born of God I know I am
    Way down in Egypt land,
I'm purchased by the dying Lamb
    Way down in Egypt land.

Peter walked upon the sea
    Way down in Egypt land,
And Jesus told him, "Come to me"
    Way down in Egypt land.[40]

As was seen in "Run, Mary, Run," a connection is made between the Exodus and Christ's Passion. A deep and robust Christology emerges in this hymn. Not only is Jesus God incarnate, he is the same God that was present with the Israelites in Egypt. Not only is there no antagonism between the person of Christ and the Old Testament, but it was Jesus himself that set the slaves free, an action that is deeply connected to his Passion. As the Apocalypse says, Jesus is "the Lamb slain from the foundation of the world" (Rev 13:8). This connection is one that is also made in Orthodox hymnography, most frequently in the first ode of the common structure of the canon, which is based on Exodus 15:1–19. The first irmos for the canon for Holy Communion reads:

> Come, O ye people, let us sing a hymn to Christ our God,
> Who divided the sea and guided the people whom He
> brought out of the bondage of Egypt, for He is glorified.[41]

In both hymns, Christ is eternal, the God of the Old Testament, and the Liberator. Through "Come Down," not only is the identity of Jesus as Israel's Liberator disclosed, but the character of the Old Testament God is revealed as continuous with the New Testament. The supposed conflict between the Old and the New Testaments was much less of an issue for American slaves because the biblical narrative was primarily understood as one of liberation, rather than legalism. This is perhaps why the theme of God's vindictive wrath against sinners is seldom present in the Spirituals. The soteriological image used most often in the Spirituals is that of the Exodus, with God understood as the one who frees His people from the oppression of injustice, sin, and death. For American slaves, the chief concern in the narrative of salvation was not accounting for a divine law that has been broken, but acquiring freedom from the chains of sin and suffering. The Orthodox Paschal troparion also testifies to this understanding of God's victory over death: "Christ is risen from the dead, trampling down death by death, and upon those in the tombs bestowing life."[42] The victory is not over "those in the tombs" that transgressed God's law, but over death itself, which held sinners captive. In Orthodox hymnography and in the African American Spirituals, God is understood as Deliverer.

In "Come Down," the use of "Egypt land" represents a state of suffering and oppression, and the hymn's pleading with God to "come down" demonstrates an understanding of Christ as a sympathetic Savior. The last verse's mention of St. Peter walking on water also reveals that the struggle for faith in the midst of doubt is also characteristic of "Egypt land." Christ is asked to descend to each of these instantiations of "Egypt," with the singer trusting in His compassion. Here, we see a unity between Christ's humanity and divinity. He is at once the God with the power to liberate, and the human with humility to identify with suffering. Another Spiritual praises Christ's humility and divine transcendence simultaneously:

He's King of Kings, and Lord of Lords,
Jesus Christ, the first and last,
    No man works like him.

He built a platform in the air,
    No man works like him.
He meets the saints from everywhere,
    No man works like him.
He pitched a tent on Canaan's ground.
    No man works like him.
And broke the Roman Kingdom down,
    No man works like him.[43]

In these lines, Christ is King, but He is also human. In the context of a life lived in hard and manual labor, the affirmation, "no man works like him," is more than a general confession of God's power—it is also a bold assertion of Christ's humanity. Unlike the Roman rulers, and unlike the slave masters, Christ was not a slothful King who relegated hard labor to his subjects. Christ was a man that worked, just as the slaves worked. Christ is a man accustomed to hard labor and suffering. In this way, Christ is understood as standing in solidarity with the human condition, which ultimately extends into the experience of death. Thurman writes,

> He suffered, He died, but not alone—they [the enslaved] were with Him. They knew what He suffered; it was a cry of the heart that found a response and an echo in their own woes. They entered into the fellowship of His suffering.[44]

So for the Spirituals, identification with Christ was reciprocal: In response to Christ's solidarity with the human condition, the enslaved also could identify with His Passion.

The slaves' proximity to Christ's sufferings is illustrated by the words of a popular Spiritual:

> Were you there when they crucified my Lord?
> Were you there when they crucified my Lord?
> Oh! Sometimes it causes me to tremble, tremble, tremble;
> Were you there when they crucified my Lord?[45]

The question is not merely rhetorical. Having witnessed and experienced deep suffering, enslaved Christians connected deeply with Christ and shared in "the fellowship of his sufferings" (Phil 3:10). It is not only the fact of Christ having suffered in solidarity with all humanity that causes one to tremble. It is the visceral connection the enslaved shared with Christ that brought a weightiness to the Passion. Through these experiences, the singers of this Spiritual were mystically transported to the Crucifixion. The enslaved understood the Passion because they *had been there*—they had seen images of His Passion in the suffering of the slave community. It was this experience of Christ's presence in suffering that transformed the cross of slavery into something salvific.

Through the Valley:
The Transformation of Suffering

AFRICAN AMERICAN SLAVES are often thought of as helpless victims, and not without good reason. They were taken against their will from their homeland and forced into a life of involuntary labor. On the one hand, the experience of slavery was a form of suffering that lacked any inherent meaning or dignity. On the other hand, the Spirituals bear witness to an experience of suffering that was transformed through fellowship with Christ. The Christian faith imbued slaves with a deep sense of moral responsibility and even an identification with Christ. As Albert Raboteau, a historian of slave religion, has observed, the occurrence of forgiveness of abusive masters in slave narratives demonstrates a sense of moral superiority and an imitation of Christ on the Cross, who said, "Forgive them, for they know not what they do."[46] In this way, enslaved Christians were not merely powerless victims, but assumed the likeness of Christ as sacrifice. The slave Martyr Ezekiel, mentioned earlier, was killed while praying for the salvation of his master. By extending forgiveness to their oppressors, the slaves transcended their victimhood and embraced their suffering as a form of spiritual sacrifice. Such a position could hardly be considered one of weakness. On the contrary, the ability to transform suffering and to even love one's enemies is one of the great and powerful mysteries of the Cross of Christ. The ability to take up the cross of suffering is made possible by following Christ Himself:

> We shall walk through the valley and the shadow of death,
> We shall walk through the valley in peace,
> If Jesus Himself shall be our leader
> We shall walk through the valley in peace.[47]

Another Spiritual makes mention of the spiritual valley of struggle and suffering, and makes it clear that it is a deeply existential and personal experience:

> I must walk my lonesome valley,
> I got to walk it for myself
> Nobody else can walk it for me,
> I got to walk it for myself.

The valley of suffering, the valley of the cross, is one that each person must choose and walk voluntarily. The final verse of this song reveals that the valley of suffering was first walked by Jesus Himself.

> Jesus walked his lonesome valley,
> He had to walk it for himself,
> Nobody else could walk it for him,
> He had to walk it for himself.[48]

The choice to walk the lonesome valley, then, is one that can be made by following Christ. As Christ said in the Gospel, "If anyone desires to come after Me, let him deny himself, and take up his cross, and follow Me" (Mt 16:24). By following Christ, the suffering under slavery becomes more than something that is involuntarily thrust upon the slave. By the cross, the experience of slavery becomes the means of transformation into the likeness of Christ.

Here it would be imprecise to speak of an American slave ascetical theology. In a certain sense, asceticism exists as a distinct and explicit category of religious experience mostly for those whose lives are not marked by suffering and struggle. Those that choose the ascetic life do so because a life of comfort is available to them. Asceticism may be distinguished from ordinary, incidental suffering in the sense that it is voluntarily assumed and by nature, intended to facilitate spiritual growth. While Christianity, and Judaism before it, always contained aspects of asceticism, those elements were formalized with the rise of monasticism after Christianity was legalized in the fourth century. From the earliest periods of Christianity, the Church prescribed ascetic practices such as fasting and withdrawal from the world, but with the rise of monasticism, there emerged Christians who dedicated their lives to prayer and renunciation of worldly pursuits. This set the standard for Christian ascetic practice in a world where Christianity enjoyed increasing popularity. So, while there is a distinction between the developed ascetic theology of Orthodox Christianity and the theology of suffering that is manifest in the African American Spirituals, some similarities may be observed.

Howard Thurman described the Spirituals' redemptive power as such:

> There is a bottomless resourcefulness in man that ultimately enables him to transform "the spear of frustration into a shaft of light." Under such a circumstance even one's deepest distress becomes so sanctified that a vast illumination points the way to the land one seeks. This is the God in man; because of it, man stands in immediate candidacy for the power to absorb all the pain of life without destroying his joy.[49]

The Spirituals contain an ascetic theology in that they are manifestations of the struggle to transform involuntary suffering into a voluntary offering to God. An example of this in ancient Christian hymnography is "O Gladsome Light."

Regarding one of the oldest recorded hymns of the Church, St. Basil the Great noted that "O Gladsome Light"

was already an old hymn by his time and credited its authorship to the Holy Martyr Athenogenes.[50]* According to St.
Basil, the Martyr Athenogenes—who was martyred during the
time of Diocletian—sang this hymn as he was approaching his
execution by fire. It is striking to note the link between
Athenogenes's method of death and the mention of light in
the ancient hymn, often accompanied by the lighting of the
evening candle or lamp. In approaching his death by immola-
tion, Athenogenes recited the lamp-lighting hymn, as if to
offer himself as the evening light of prayer. A parallel might
be drawn to the words of St. Ignatius of Antioch, who, in approaching his own martyrdom, likened his body to wheat that
would be ground down into eucharistic bread.[51] The Martyrs
of the Church often understood their bodies to be offered in
voluntary sacrifice to God, as opposed to victims of their exe-
cutioners. In the cases of St. Ignatius and Martyr Athenogenes, both saints responded to their suffering with praise to
God. What is more, both saints actually transformed what
could be understood as involuntary victimization into a voluntary "sacrifice of praise." In the case of Ignatius, he offered
his body in the same manner that he would offer the Eucharist in his priestly office. For the Martyr Athenogenes, his
body became the light illumining the evening prayer, which
he offered in the form of a hymn that is still sung in the Vespers service to this day. The martyrdoms of Ignatius and
Athenogenes were the means by which they worshipped God.

A comparison can be made to the new martyrs and confessors of American slavery, especially those that were persecuted specifically for their observance of the faith. Though their
sufferings were involuntary and thrust upon them, through
the composition of the sorrow songs, those sufferings were
transformed into an offering to God. In the case of Athenogenes, his persecution produced one of the most time-
honored hymns of the Christian faith. The case of the slave

---

* Some Orthodox liturgical books credit the hymn to St. Sophronius, Patriarch of Jerusalem. He may, in fact, have revised it.

Spirituals is a similar story in that their suffering produced hymns that have encouraged many Christians beyond their own experience. The Spirituals of the American slaves are the embodiment of profound and deep faith, and they remain as witnesses to a theological tradition forged in struggle.

Conclusion

I BEGAN THIS CHAPTER by examining the ways that I had been impacted by the American slave Spirituals, and the ways that I had been unfairly critical of them. In the years that I have been Orthodox, I have had the pleasure of hearing many of these Spirituals sung para-liturgically in several Orthodox churches. For many years, it was a local custom in the parish where I was received into the Church to sing "Wade in the Water" after a Baptism.* I have also heard many of the Spirituals mentioned in this chapter sung during gatherings at conferences for the Fellowship of St. Moses the Black. Hearing these songs sung by Orthodox Christians, surrounded by icons of Christ, the Theotokos, and the saints, I felt as though the Spirituals began to harmonize with the hymns and the theology of the Orthodox Church. When I heard these songs in this context, surrounded by the lives of so many martyrs of the Faith, I understood immediately how much they resonated with the theology of the Orthodox Church. These songs, as I have tried to demonstrate, contain themes that are very much at home in the Orthodox story. Though they have suffered great misinterpretation, when read in the context of the suffering slave community, they reveal deep and profound theological truths. And when compared to the witness of the Orthodox Faith, they find much in common with the witness of Orthodox hymnography.

The Spirituals were written by a people who, in many ways, had much more in common than I with the saints and martyrs of the Orthodox Church. The Spirituals were the

---

* See Hieromonk Alexii Altschul's chapter in this volume, p. 3.

fruit of the heavy cross of involuntary suffering, transformed by faith into a sacrifice of praise that comprises the best of the spiritual legacy of this country. They were the cry of the oppressed to a God that liberates. They were the melodies that energized the striving for justice in this fallen world. They were the choruses of deep spiritual longing birthed in the caves of many broken hearts. If we have the spiritual ears to hear them, the Spirituals continue to be sung in that land beyond the Jordan, beckoning us to join them in singing the Lord's song.

3

CALLING
DOWN
THE HOLY SPIRIT
AFRICAN AMERICAN
HYMNOGRAPHY

FR. MOSES BERRY

S WEETEST JESUS SAVE US! My name is Father Moses Berry and I live in the house that my great grandparents built in 1871 in the Ozark Mountains of Missouri. My spiritual tradition is AME Zion Methodist. I'm a third generation AME pastor's son and I live in the house that they built. My great grandfather built that house. My grandfather was born and raised in that house. My father was born and raised in that house. I was born and raised in this house. And now I've raised my children there, although now they have flown the coop. And when we speak about my tradition and linking this Orthodox liturgical tradition with African American Gospel music, I first ask myself which African American Gospel are you referring to? Because we are so much broader than we sometimes let ourselves believe. St. Nikolai Velimirovich says our religion is founded on spiritual experience seen and heard as pure as any physical fact in the world. Not theory, not philosophy, not human emotion but experience—in our experience, in the African American church in America as it was founded by God Almighty.

My great grandfather was a slave in the area that we now live. He had three masters during his lifetime, and two of his masters' families live only a mile from my house. All the experiences that he had concerning the church came directly from God just as many of the African American expressions come directly from God Almighty. I was raised in a church where my mother painted the murals on the wall from the life of Christ—life-sized murals on the wall in some kind of iconographic fashion. And so, we were born and raised in that situation. I became disillusioned during the turbulent 1960s when this church that we embraced so dearly became just like every other church. After this integration we no longer had to rely on the kindness and the fair-mindedness of people around us and the protection from God. We were forced into having fairness come to us by way of the court system. And I went all around this country trying to find that missing piece, that missing piece that connected my heart and my life to that so-called old-time religion. And I could not find it in the way that it expressed itself in my youth.

At one point my wife and I became non-denominational pastors and we went to visit a friend of ours because many of our friends around us were becoming Orthodox. I said I will never become Orthodox because that is not the religion of my ancestors. We were invited to visit our friend in Richmond, Virginia. And so, we drove down the road from Atlanta, Georgia. Reluctantly, I drove and we got to that place to this church house which was actually a little bit of a two story building. And we went up the stairs and I was disturbed because I didn't like that building. It didn't remind me of a church. I went inside that church and there was a three-person choir. Now I know it was probably the priest, his wife, and one of the faithful parishioners. And I said to my wife with no respect, out loud, "This isn't even a real choir." And then I heard the choir and it sang, "Rejoice thou through whom joy will flash forth. Rejoice revival of fallen Adam. Rejoice redemption of the tears of Eve. Rejoice thou Bride unwedded." And it cut me to the quick.

I actually thought that they were speaking in a foreign language because I didn't know that you could put words together in such a way. Something from the eternal touched my life and I knew that the very sound that was being produced in an Orthodox Church was the same sound that was being produced in my soul during my youth. There's a certain resonance in all worship music if it's genuinely done and born out of suffering.

Evangelism Through Music

WE HAVE AN ALL-AMERICAN COUNCIL, a gathering of people from our Orthodox tradition in the Orthodox Church in America. And in 2011 I submitted a resolution. The resolution reads like this:

> Whereas there is a deep resonance between the faith of the Early Church and the heartfelt Christianity born out of the African American slave experience especially characterized by the sad joyfulness common to the desert fathers and mothers and the suffering underground church of the African American slaves; whereas African Americans have been and are still significantly underrepresented in the holy, catholic, and apostolic Church in America; we are therefore resolved that the Orthodox Church in America at every level of Church life promote and encourage education about the shared heritage of black and white Americans, and the necessity to increase the efforts to evangelize.

One of the ways for sure that we evangelize is through the sound that we make, the sound that we make that resonates throughout our soul.

I CAME BACK to the country, back to my hometown after being away for so many years. And I thought, well these people won't even know me anymore. But all the old folks loved me. All those old people from the AME church, my mother's contemporaries and my grandmother's contemporaries gathered in our cemetery for slaves, Indians, and paupers which is on the National Historic Sites Registry of Historic Places. We have three Osage Indian Mounds there, and some of Harriet Tubman's people are buried in our cemetery, in particular, Mother Charity. We went back there to the cemetery. We had been living in St. Louis, the big city, and when my family and I came back to the Ozarks we decided to have a prayer service in the cemetery. And when we were there we sang this particular Orthodox song to the Mother of God and for the departed; for those who had departed, those that lost their lives and had no one to pray for them, those who were under harsh labor and had no one to release their bonds. When we finished singing this song my great aunt Willetta, a daughter of a slave (I was also raised by the daughter of a slave. I was born only eighty five years after the Civil War). My great aunt Willetta said "That sounds just like the way the old folks used to sing." And I said to myself, "Oh they loved me so much they just want to agree with me on this thing. They want to include me."

Later I realized that it wasn't a matter of inclusion. It was a matter of a soul experience because those words, especially the words that say "The wise children did not adore the golden idol but went themselves into the flames and defied the pagan gods, they prayed in the midst of the flames and an angel was there with them; the prayer of our lips has been heard." When we sing such things as that in the Orthodox tradition it resonates in our soul, as we often say, the soul of the black man. It resonates in the soul of all men because it speaks to a condition that we suffer from. So, I was pleased to know that even my daughter who is a great singer and taught this ethnomusicology at Harvard had something underneath all that that resonated.

People ask me sometimes, how can we make a bridge with African American Gospel music? And this is what I always say: You get African American people together and have them sing in a liturgical fashion and you will have liturgical African American music. My great grandmother, who was a choir director and a singer, longed for the days when she could be connected to the ancient tradition. I know she did because she would lead us to the front porch of their house and she would tell us that there was something more to reach for. And she would teach us not to judge people for how they looked, or how much money they had. She would say, "now I have something to say to you," and she would recite a poem to the children. It's by Paul Laurence Dunbar— "The Party." Paul Laurence Dunbar was born in Dayton, Ohio, and he became an elevator operator in Dayton, and he would recite his poetry to people that were going up and down the hand-operated elevator and someone said "Oh my goodness, he must be a real poet!" They thought they had discovered him, but the African American community had long since discovered him. Paul Laurence Dunbar's poem "The Party" begins by two women talking over a clothesline about this party that five plantations were invited to. And during this conversation the ladies started talking about this wonderful party, and how one got to go and the other did not go. She talked about all the wonderful things they got to eat, the candied yams and so on and all this beautiful and lovely fare. And now I will paraphrase this poem. I won't use the Negro dialect that Paul Laurence Dunbar uses but I'll put it in modern Ozark language: When they finished eating the fiddler got up on the floor so they could dance that dinner down, and the saints and the sinners were so mixed up on that floor, That I'm sure God could not have separated them if the trumpets had chanced to blow.[1] This inner sameness, not the outer sameness resonates between us all—the same broken-heartedness that we experience in our church music, whether it be East or West or in between. The same broken-heartedness speaks of that

43

which Jesus came for—to heal the broken-hearted, to set at liberty those who were bruised, to preach the acceptable year of the Lord (cf. Lk 4:18, 19). That resonates within all of us.

WHEN I FIRST MET the people from Reconciliation Ministries and they told me that they wanted to be Orthodox, I continually told the pastor, David—now he's Fr. Alexii—"It would be a good idea, but you should not become Orthodox at the cost of giving up Reconciliation Ministries. I would rather that you stay the way that you are than become Orthodox." It was obvious to me that the Spirit of God was upon them. And that's what makes someone Orthodox. Fr. Damascene—along with other knowledgeable people—talks about the high spiritual level of the African American Spirituals and Gospel music.*[2] I know that if you want to be Orthodox, in fact, you have to know that you're not a citizen of this world. The Gospel that we're talking about in this chapter, the Gospel music and the Spiritual music, which are two different forms, are born from people who knew that they were not of this world. As a matter of fact, they knew it to the degree that they wouldn't even be accepted as citizens in this world. They were far from it. The cemetery on our property was made for people who were not of this world. Some of them, of course, were not Christians, but many of them were. And it was made for those people who knew that they were not citizens of this world.

When the slaves were freed, from after the Civil War, they didn't know what to do. They were released into a world where they weren't citizens and where they weren't able to exercise any freedom at all. So, they had to develop their own worldview. For many African Americans the worldview that they developed was the Gospel. If you want to know how you ought to act in certain situations, you had to refer to the Gospels:

---

* See Abbot Damascene Christensen's chapter, p. 60 of this volume, and his section on African American Spirituals in *Foundations: 1994–1997*, pp. 142–145.

Matthew, Mark, Luke, and John and ask yourself, what would Jesus do and what does He say? Where does He say His kingdom is? And where does He say His kingdom is from? Well, that's why when I listen to Gospel music, I listen to church music. I don't find it to be a form of entertainment at all. It's not something that we sing in order to hear our voices or to listen to African American folk music. I have a CD at home by Paul Robeson called *Spirituals/Folksongs/Hymns*[3]—he breaks it down into those three categories. Now folksongs, ballads, and such are meant to entertain. But Spirituals and Gospel hymns are meant to bring down the Holy Spirit.

Now we have to respect ourselves a little bit, respect our heritage, when we listen to an Akathist to the Mother of God. We know that as a result of singing these songs, that there will be a pouring out of the Holy Spirit. When we sing songs like an Akathist for the Departed, or a moleben,* we do this for the sole purpose of bringing down the Holy Spirit, and beseeching God to enter into our life. The same is true in both Spiritual music, and Gospel music.

For when I lived among white people for the last many years, I had never told anyone about Gospel music, because I was afraid they would start tapping their feet and clapping their hands and they might think this is a form of entertainment—not really making a mockery, because these were my friends and they never would. But it's not a form of entertainment. It's a way of bringing the Holy Spirit upon this earth and reminding us that we are not of this world. That's the purpose of Gospel music. It almost can't be sung anymore. Not real Gospel music. People sing certain things, nowadays, but now we also know that we're citizens of this world, and we have to sort of get by in this world, one way or another. So the genuine essence of the Gospel music is gone. It's not dead, because we can revamp it, and that's what I'm hoping to do. I'm hoping to revitalize the whole Gospel

---

* An Orthodox prayer service, usually petitioning God for help with an urgent need. It may also be done in thanksgiving.

movement that came about at the turn of the century when people were just released from slavery. And many people had gone to Northern cities and left the cotton fields or the workforce in the South where they sang those Spirituals and went up North and began to sing Gospel music. But they also knew that they were not of this world.

Theology of Experience

SO, I'M GOING TO TALK about various musical forms that we find in Gospel music. The first form of Gospel music is called the theology of experience. When we learn about Gospel music and how it's affected a whole group of people, we have to realize it was because it was their theology. Not a theology that came from seminary, although seminary theology is good. Many of these people couldn't even read. I remember my grandmother telling me that the men from the railroad used to come to her house because she could read and write and they wanted her to write letters home to their loved ones. And my grandmother told me one story about this fellow from Texas who said, "I want you to write this love letter to my girlfriend," (or wife, whoever she was), "but I want to put some cotton in your ears, because I don't want you to hear it." These people were not exactly ready for Main Street. They lived in another world. Those people existed, and I remember them. I was fortunate enough to be born in this time—eighty years after the end of slavery. People who were alive in my childhood could have been slaves—the children of slaves. Even some people that I knew as a boy, when I was maybe five years old were once slaves. And they were a different breed. I remember not wanting to ever go home again. I would run away from my home almost every night to go to my grandmother's house. Finally they gave up on me, and just said, "Stay out there." That's where I live today, in her house. They were a different breed. Their home was not in this world. That's where Gospel music comes from. It comes from a hope not of this world, a hope that is beyond this world. You know all the songs that say,

"Look away beyond the blue"? You know the one that goes, "Do Lord, Oh, do Lord, do remember me, Look away beyond the blue." What do you think we were referring to? Looking away beyond this world, because there will be no satisfaction in this world. That's theology.

The theology of experience has to do with how people are mistreated in life and what they hope for. And it comes from direct experience. From trying God, and knowing that the only help that is possible is the help that God can bring. Now I want to tell you about a particular song, about the experience of not looking to this world. It's by a group called the Fairfield Four,* one of my favorite new groups—newly discovered groups. I know that we used to sing songs from the Fairfield Four when I was a boy. I always sang Gospel music, since I was a little boy. I remember the first time that we sang in church. My grandmother sprang it on us. She got up, and this was in the AME church, and she said, "Now my grandsons are going to sing a song for us." Of course, this was totally unannounced. My brother and I were just cutting up. (This lady today told me that her son was running around there, and I thought, "Well my goodness, if she'd only seen my brother and me running around!" We were jumping up and down on the pews in my grandfather's church.) You know, my brother and I were just cutting up, and all of a sudden this woman jumped up behind us boys, grabbed us by the collar, and said "unleash them, Satan!" Because she knew the only reason I could be acting like that. She believed in the Gospel, but I didn't. I'm only just now beginning to believe in the Gospel again. Believe in it in the sense that it is my life. And that's the only life and only hope that I have.

So, this song by the Fairfield Four is called "My God Called Me This Morning." And we know it's truly Gospel music because the effect it has on us is like liturgical music. It moves

---

* The Fairfield Four is a Gospel band that started in 1921 at the Fairfield Baptist Church and has existed for over 90 years. Some of their performances can be heard on YouTube.

you in a place that's a little bit different than the feeling of just wanting to clap your hands. It moves you in your soul, on such a level that makes you want to know God. It makes you want to understand your relationship to Him and to abandon the world. That's what Gospel music does, the same as any other church music that we sing. I know this to be the case.

WE CONSECRATED OUR CEMETERY—not that it needed to be consecrated, because people had been buried there since 1875. We wanted to have an Orthodox cemetery, a place where Orthodox people could officially be buried, so we consecrated the cemetery. And people in there were singing songs to the Mother of God. So how do you explain the Mother of God to someone? One way to explain the Mother of God is in song. When the sisters began to sing the Akathist to the Mother of God, then my mother and aunts and the old people said, "That sounds just like Gospel music." Well, I don't think it does exactly. But it reminded me of another time that I was with an Ethiopian priest. We were in California at a baptism and it was a chilly day. We went down to the rushing river and we baptized these men. The Ethiopian priest said, "You know what? This reminds me of Ethiopia." I've never been to Ethiopia, but it doesn't sound Ethiopian. But something reminded him of that. It was the other-worldliness of the occasion. This same other-worldliness is what reminded my mother and my aunts of Gospel music. She said, "This really sounds like Gospel music." This is a woman who knew music. They sang in choirs, and actually their radio recordings are in the archives at Branson, Missouri for Gospel singers. They had a radio show and they were on every Sunday, rain or shine. And they were great. They won't let me handle those copies from the archives. I'm still working on it. The thing that reminded my people—that made them think that this music was like Orthodox music—was because something from the eternal touched their lives when they heard it. And that's why I also sing Gospel music, but I only sing it in church. Gospel music is church music. And unless we raise it to that rank of church music, then it will become entertainment.

I WAS INVITED TO A CHURCH to give a little talk on Gospel music and the African American experience and that is where I met Fr. Roman Braga.* He was a Romanian monk and had been in concentration camps under Ceausescu. He was tortured and they did all sorts of things to him. I went into the church and there was a young priest serving the Liturgy there. He didn't cense me. I was back in the corner in the back of the church and I started feeling a little bit bad, you know. I am a human, barely, sometimes. He wouldn't even cense me. Fr. Roman took off his vestments and came out of the altar. He came back and stood beside me, and said, "If they won't cense you, they won't cense me." And of course, that was a great lesson to me, and a prelude to what he told me. Later that morning when we had breakfast he said, "You know, you have to find a way of developing a liturgical music that speaks to the African American people." I told him, "Fr. Roman, it's already there. We just have to find a way to integrate it in the Church." And so that was some confirmation for me, to hear someone outside of my immediate circle of friends that found agreement with what I thought. Not that it would validate my thinking, but it made me think that perhaps this was something beyond my own imagination. We're talking about the theology of experience. Do you understand what I mean so far by "the theology of experience"? Those things that impact your life, when you're walking down the road and your heart is breaking, and you say, "I just wish I had someone to depend on"—all these laments that the human soul cries out. This has to do with our

---

* Fr. Roman Braga (1922–2015) was a Romanian priest-monk who spent time in Romanian prisons and later was sent to Brazil and later to America. He eventually retired to Holy Dormition Monastery in Michigan.

experience. The theology of experience is how the teachings and the word of Jesus impact our personal experience. You can choose to go walking down the road with or without God.

FROM THE SAME TIME PERIOD, 1937, when the Fairfield Four recorded this song, there was also another man who made a record. It was a secular version of what happens to you when you walk down the road and you feel bad. It's almost the truth. But it's not quite there, because it doesn't have Jesus in it. This is a recording that may be familiar to some of you, by Champion Jack Dupree. Well, that's the blues. The blues brings us very close to being on our knees. It doesn't quite do it, but it brings us right to the brink, because it describes the human condition. We're talking about Gospel music, these were sung by people who were treated all sorts of ways. These were people who had worn neck irons, enslaved only a few years earlier. Then they would walk down the streets and people would spit in their faces and do all kinds of things to them. It was just horrible. But it's only horrible if you don't have God. If you have God then you can take your burdens to the Lord and leave them there. You know that song, don't you? "Take your burden to the Lord, leave it there." That's what the Gospel tradition is based on: how this world impacts us and what we do with it. There is a difference between Gospel and blues—they're very close, you know. One is with God, and the other is without God. Blues is such a beautiful form; it's born from the same longing that Gospel music is born from, it just doesn't include God. "I wonder what is going on," and "I don't have a friend, I wish I had a friend" is what he's saying in the blues song I just described earlier. The Gospel tradition says, "The only friend I have is Jesus." "I have no friends in this world but Jesus." Big difference. One is hopeless, and one is full of hope. But it's almost the same thing. It's born out of the same suffering, the same heartbreak, but there's no hope in the blues.

Theology of Imagination

NOW THE GOLDEN GATE QUARTET* shows the theology of imagination—the second kind of Gospel music that we have. It grew out of what Al Raboteau calls "fire in the bones." We have this stirring deep within us, and it makes us want to shout. It used to make me somewhat embarrassed, because I wanted to be a citizen of the world. I'd see these people who didn't have any hope, but in God, and they would be shouting in church and they would be doing things. We did get very happy about the whole idea of God being in our life, and people would shout and testify. And I remember the last time I saw my grandmother, Dorothy—my daughter, Dorothy,† is named after her. I went to a church, it was called the Donovan Chapel in Jefferson City, Missouri, and I went there to preach a sermon. They asked because I was a newly ordained minister and they thought, "We have to test his mettle." I mean that's what they were thinking because they gave instruction before I started, "Don't preach too long—just get to the truth of it." And I remember I started talking about my personal experience. And one woman named Bridget Wingo jumps up in the back of the church and she said, "You know we're the cause of your conversion because we saw you doing those little ornery things around here and prayed for you. This is a direct result of our prayers, our prayers for your conversion." I was only 23 years old. You know that's young, you don't have enough experience to say amen. That kind of theology of imagination that makes them believe that their prayer has effect and is long lasting. And then when they begin to imagine this then they begin to realize that the truth of God is there. It's not the imagination as in a daydream, but as a man thinketh so he becomes (cf. Prov 23:7).

---

* Golden Gate Quartet was begun in 1934 by four students of Booker T. Washington High School in Nashville, TN. They became well known and recorded frequently into the 1950s. In '62 they did a tour of Africa and became popular in Europe. They had a 60-year anniversary performance in 1994.

† Dorothy Berry is the Digital Curator for the National Museum of African American History and Culture. She received her MLS from Indiana University, as well as an MA in Ethnomusicology from the same institution.

Now we imagine that someday we will lay down our burdens. That's what this theology of imaginations is—of knowing that someday this labor will be over. That's the whole meaning of the Gospel and of Gospel music. Let's not think any longer of Gospel music being some sort of art form. Let's look at it as a theological idea of how we live our lives according to the Gospel. I refuse and I encourage you to also reject the idea that Gospel music is anything less than how to get to heaven. That's what it's all about even though recent singers have great voices, like Shirley Caesar or Reverend Andraé Crouch. Dr. Carla and I used to sing his music. We used to go in the lounge at Harvard Medical School and play it on the piano. He could sing, but there's something he didn't do. He didn't transmit that idea that this world does not count. That's a hard thing to understand, especially for me because I would rather have a Mercedes than a Ford. I don't get either one, but I'd rather have a Mercedes. It's hard to forsake this world entirely. And these people who brought us the Gospel tradition that we so fondly refer to, did not have any hope in this world.

I remember being a little boy before they had integrated bathrooms. I remember going to see my grandmother at the Lake of the Ozarks. We drove through Missouri. We caught a little bus and stopped at a Conoco station. I was about five, and my brother was about six and we had to go to the bathroom. We came in and my mother got off the bus with us and then there's a colored sign. And we said, "We have to go now, Mom!" And she said, "Well you can't. You have to wait." So I said, "We're going to go on ourselves if we're not careful." She said, "What you have to do is ask Jesus to help you." She gave us the other-worldly alternative. The other-worldly alternative is to trust in the Lord. I remember we used to take these road trips down the highway. And I was always amazed that my relatives would stop along the side of the highway and they would go up in the woods a little bit and relieve themselves. I thought they were so strange. I was an innocent boy, I didn't know—I guessed they liked it. And I was speaking to my mom about it in later years and she said, "Well you know we couldn't use the bathrooms." They were not resentful. Some people were of course, but other people said, "By and by little children, by and by, I'm going to lay down my burden by and by." That's the message of Gospel music. That's how we were taught how the Lord works in our lives. You have to remember that we, the African Americans, come from a very long and proud tradition of people who sang their way to heaven.

We used to say, "Oh we can't sing" and my grandmother would say, "Just make a joyful noise to the Lord so He can hear you." There's this story about how God makes people Orthodox. This is a story about a man who was a slave. And then something from the eternal touched his life. God moved on the water as they say, and he was freed from the bondage of his hatreds. The master decided to punish him and tied him up to a tree. This is the power of the Holy Spirit, if you know the Gospel of our Lord Jesus Christ. Hopefully you know a few things about Gospel music. Jesus told of a man who could not even so much as lift up his eyes to heaven and he hit his breast and said, "Lord have mercy on me a sinner." You remember that? And the Gospel says that the pharisee who says, "I'm okay, and I'm trying hard, fasting," and it was sincere, and he was actually doing those things. So we don't accuse him. But there was one thing he lacked because he judged his brother. He thought himself better and higher than his brother. And so Jesus said that the first man went down to his house that day justified rather than the other (see Lk 18:10–14). St. Isaac the Syrian says that justification is the forgiveness of sins. His sins were forgiven him and the other man's, were not. As I was saying, they were beating this slave with a whip and every time he would come to, they would bring the lash across his back in a terrible way and beat him till his bones were bare, and he would say, "Lord have mercy on me a sinner." Who taught this man to say the Jesus

Prayer? Isn't this an Orthodox tradition? Isn't this the Orthodox highest spiritual practice? The Holy Spirit made many of our righteous ancestors Orthodox—that is, to have the right view, the right outlook. So many of our ancestors were Christian men and women who suffered. They were actually Orthodox according to Jesus Christ. We can say that we've been born again in Jesus Christ and we asked the question how can a man a second time enter into his mother's womb and be born. And we know that we go to the river as the song says and we are baptized. It's the imagination—I think we should call it the hope or the faith but it is referred to often as the imagination—this hope and faith of that which is to come.

Theology of Grace

THE NEXT IDEA of this theology that we'll speak of is the theology of grace. You all know the singer of my generation, Stevie Wonder. Stevie Wonder says, "You brought some joy inside my tears."[4] Do you remember that song? "You have done what no one thought could be; you brought some joy inside my tears." And in another song he said, "if it's special, then why aren't we as careful with it." He is referring to love. "It holds the key to every heart, throughout the universe, it fills you up without a bite, quenches every thirst, so if it's special then why aren't we more careful." This has to do with the theology of grace and the Gospel songs. Stevie Wonder was very torn, like other musicians of our time. He was torn between being a Gospel singer and making his way into secular songs. Very few people have been able to do that, even people who are called by God. We know how it is to be called by God and we say, "Yes Jesus, I'll come," and then something happens and you don't come. Sometimes we play like we came, but we really didn't. We believe we have professed we loved Christ, but didn't follow Him. I'm sure that you have done this—or perhaps you haven't. If you haven't then please pray for me. I might be subject to this again. The theology of grace brings forth hope out of a situation that is hopeless; it brings joy where there is no joy. Do you know they've talked about the Hebrew children in the fiery furnace and how they danced around in the flame and sang songs, and we sing their song every time we have the Matins service, we sing the Praises. Did you know that? We sing the Praises in Matins, "All the things in creation help me." That's giving thanks and praise for every single thing that happens in your life. That's the song that the Hebrew children sang in the midst of flames. An angel bestowed grace upon them and kept them from harm. And that's the whole idea of the theology of grace. In the Gospel tradition, when we are in the midst of losing, when we're in the midst of this terrible situation that causes us to dance in the flame, how shall we behave? What shall we sing?

Matushka Michaila told me I have to speak on this. I told her one time that I will not speak of these ideas about the African American Orthodox tradition as it relates to the black Gospel music because someone might trample them. But she said, "You have to do it." Blind Willie Johnson* had a very hard time. His mother died and he didn't know what to do. His father got remarried, but his wife turned out to be a mean stepmother. And she would get so mad that she would just drop him off in town and leave him there. He didn't have any babysitters or friends to look after him. And so he stood under an awning out of the sun and rain and he would sing Gospel music all day long. He played his little guitar he had made out of a box, and pulled the strings. He had a cup around his neck. He became a great preacher. All his messages were, "Love those who despise you, use you and say all manner of evil against you for My Name" (cf. Mt 5:11). That's the Gospel music. He loved God with all his heart all his life. He had a sad death. He had pneumonia, and he went to the hospital but they wouldn't take him in at the hospital, and he prayed and sang songs on his dying bed. It reminded me of

---

* Blind Willie Johnson (1897–1945) was a Gospel and blues singer, evangelist and street performer.

the Gospel song that was, "I looked over the Jordan and I said Jesus I'm making up my dying bed."

NOW I WANT TO TALK about a song by the Five Blind Boys of Alabama.* The song is sort of disturbing. It kind of reminds me of iconography because if you listen to it, and if you study it a little bit, you can be taken away. It's shocking to me, and it should be to you too. Who can say they can look through a window into heaven and everything will be alright? And who can say I look at a window into heaven and I was in joy? I find this quality also in Blind Willie Johnson's music. It's a particular kind of music and they call it Panhandle Gospel, a kind of Gospel music that came out in a certain area of the United States. This is one of the most famous songs. It was written by the person that was responsible for the whole revival of Gospel music in the '20s and '30s. Thomas Dorsey† was a great songwriter. My daughter Dorothy says that he wasn't exactly the one that we should be looking to. We should be looking to Charles Tindley.‡ He brought Dorsey to the Lord through Gospel music. Dorsey began as a jazz and blues singer. Once he gave a performance in Chicago at a big Baptist church and sang one of his songs that every church sings now. My wife was raised by a nanny named Ellen who lived in Harlem. When my wife and I began courting when we lived in Harlem, I went to Ellen's house because she wanted to check me out to make sure my intentions were honorable. I went there and Ellen

---

* The group Five Blind Boys of Alabama was founded in 1939. Most of its members were visually impaired. They performed and recorded internationally.

† Thomas Dorsey (1899–1993) was an American musician, composer and evangelist who composed perhaps thousands of songs. A significant number of them were Gospel. Not to be confused with jazz musician Tommy Dorsey.

‡ Charles Albert Tindley (1851–1933) was a self-educated Methodist minister and Gospel music composer.

said, "Well, just sit down here and I'll play a little something for you." The hot seat! To see if I ran out of the building shouting! So she put on one of Dorsey's songs, "Precious Lord." That was the best song in the whole world.

> Precious Lord, take my hand
> Lead me on, let me stand
> I'm tired, I'm weak, I'm worn.
> Through the storm, through the night,
> Lead me Lord, to the light
> Take my hand, precious Lord
> Lead me home.

Dorsey wrote the song in 1932 after his wife and child died in childbirth. He felt so bad, it broke his heart. What could happen but depression? Well, one thing did—his conversion. This is the whole idea of Gospel music. He said, "How will I get out of this mess that I've gotten myself into? Precious Lord take my hand, lead me on, let me stand." Then he heard this voice from God saying, "I will." That's what we sing out to the Lord, we sing "Help me because I can't, this is impossible." And they call this the theology of survival. That's how we're able to endure. There's another Gospel music, there's white Gospel music. I have a recording from the Watson family. It's a new release on Smithsonian records. The name of the song is "I've Endured; Lord Knows I've Endured." It tells about a man saying to the Lord, "I've endured, I'm tired, I'm weak, I am worn, let me get out of here if there's any chance, with as little pain as possible"—as we say as we live our life.

My mother was dying and we didn't want her to, because we loved her. And we were with her in the hospital and she said, "Oh man I'm tired. I'm just so tired." We knew what she was talking about. It wasn't the kind of tired like she's had a long day or even a long life. It was like, "I am tired of the struggle." This reminds me of Jesus saying, "If it be at all possible, take this cup from me" (Mt 26:39). That's the whole spirit of the song—the idea of survival.

I'll close with some thoughts on the Fairfield Four. Garrison Keillor once discovered them, and he said, "Well we've got a new group here and we're going to make you famous," in other words we're going to make you some money. There's nothing wrong with that, money is how we get along until the Lord comes, right? We have to do something to get by. And He provides that. But the Fairfield Four said, "No, we won't be famous, we won't be rich, but we'll record a record for you." They recorded this song in Nashville Tennessee. This is the epitome of Gospel music because it talks about what happens to us when we leave this world. The Gospel says if the Lord should come will He know me? One song that exemplifies this is "Row, Children, Row," and "Standing in the Safety Zone" is another example. This is actually a term many old people used when they had to stand in the midst of a storm. People used to say this to me all the time. They never ever lost faith, even though they had every reason to. That's a fact. I don't know if I could be strong enough to endure what they endured, with my own children. I hope that I would have the faith, but I don't know; I haven't been tested. When I did all kinds of things growing up, crying, they would say are you standing in the safety zone? When I went to the penitentiary they would say, are you standing in the safety zone? That's Gospel music and I know it's Gospel music because it speaks about the Lord Jesus Christ and how He can deliver you from anything and anyone. You know it's Gospel music if it says, "Lord I'm tired, Lord help me, Lord I can't give up."

I'm waiting for an inspired African American young person who can help develop this idea of liturgical music so we can incorporate it in our liturgical practice. If we don't do that it could be lost forever. We need someone to help us who has a tone, not one of the eight tones, but a tone for the African American people. It's just folk music, like the Russian or the Greek music. And it has to be universal for everybody just as my relatives said that the Russian tones sound like Gospel music. So, you keep your eye out for some musical people so we can begin to train them so they can embody the spirit of African American Gospel music. It can't be contrived. It can't be made up. I think we can raise that person up, don't you? Keep your eyes out and we can help them develop music for us.

4

ORTHODOX PATRISTIC THEMES
IN AFRICAN AMERICAN GOSPEL SONGS OF THE GOLDEN AGE

ABBOT DAMASCENE CHRISTENSEN

I N THE PREVIOUS VOLUME in this series, *Foundations*, I wrote of the miracle of the Spirituals created by African Americans during the time of slavery. Here we will explore the black American religious music produced during the subsequent era, known as the age of segregation, or "Jim Crow."

After discussing some of the great singer/songwriters who lived between the emancipation of the slaves and World War II, I will especially highlight Gospel music of the Golden Age. This era is commonly regarded as having lasted from 1945 to 1960. However, there were many great singers from the Golden Age who continued to produce outstanding music through the 1970s and 1980s, and some continued to record into the 1990s.

Later in this chapter, I will compare writings by ancient Holy Fathers of the Orthodox Church with the lyrics of African American Gospel songs, in order to show how closely the two reflect each other, despite the vast differences in their respective cultural milieus.

HISTORICAL BACKGROUND

The Early Church

IN ORDER TO ILLUMINATE the commonality between 20th century African American Gospel and Patristic wisdom from ancient times, it will be helpful to provide some historical context.

During the first three centuries after our Lord Jesus Christ completed His redemptive work in Jerusalem, the Church was persecuted, not only in Jerusalem but all over the Roman Empire. In many places, Christians had to live in hiding. In the imperial city of Rome, they actually lived underground, in the catacombs. They knew that they could be captured at any time, and then tortured and killed for their Faith. Thus, during those first centuries, Christianity was anything but a comfortable Faith. The early Christians understood that the Church thrived spiritually amid persecution, for they experienced the Lord most deeply when they suffered for His sake. There's even a saying from these early centuries: that the blood of the martyrs is the seed of the Church.

In A.D. 313, the emperors St. Constantine I and Licinius issued an edict of toleration (known as the Edict of Milan), which stated that the Christian Church would no longer be persecuted in the Roman Empire. However, even though they now enjoyed legal status within the empire, Christians endured persecution due to the heresies that periodically attacked the Church. Islam, which was viewed as a heresy by the Orthodox Holy Fathers, was from its inception a scourge upon the Church. In more recent times, Christians endured the heavy yoke of atheistic Communism.

While enduring hardship from outside forces, Orthodox Christians throughout the ages have also taken on voluntary suffering for Christ's sake. After the legalization of Christianity, this was seen most obviously in the movement of men and women to deserts, forests, and other uninhabited places, there to draw closer to God in poverty and affliction, praying for the whole world and providing spiritual consolation to those who visited them. But it was not only monks and nuns who practiced ascetic discipline. From the time of Christ unto today, Orthodox Christians from all walks of life have taken on ascetic labors, especially those of prayer, fasting, and almsgiving.

African America

WITH THIS EXAMINATION of the involuntary and voluntary suffering endured by Christians from the beginning, we are now ready to look at the African American experience in its wider Christian context.

When African people were first brought to America as slaves, they of course did not know English. But more than that, they often did not know the languages of their fellow Africans, since the enslaved peoples were taken from different countries and tribes. How could they express their grief, their pain over everything that they were experiencing? They came to do so through moaning. More than plaintive cries, these moans were usually accompanied by a melody. They were sometimes communal and at other times private. The point was that, in moaning, the believers could raise their hurting hearts to God and reach out to Him wordlessly. In expressing their suffering through moaning, they found joy in the midst of it—the same joy that, as our Lord said, cannot be taken away from us by anyone (cf. Jn 16:22).

The tradition of moaning remained part of African American Christian culture for centuries after the slaves learned the English language and thus the original purpose of moaning no longer applied.

In most places of the antebellum South, slave masters did not allow their slaves to learn to read. Some of them ostensibly provided moral instruction to those under their yoke, but they presented a distorted form of the Christian Faith, designed to keep their fellow human beings in chains. Under such conditions, it was miraculous that the slaves discovered for themselves the true meaning of the Christian message. Like true Christians throughout the ages, they found that their faith in Christ not only made their suffering bearable, but brought them joy in the midst of pain. They saw fulfilled in themselves the words of our Lord Jesus Christ:

> Blessed are the poor in spirit, for theirs is the Kingdom of Heaven. Blessed are they that mourn, for they shall be comforted.... Blessed are they which are persecuted for righteousness' sake, for theirs is the Kingdom of Heaven. Blessed are ye, when men shall revile you, and persecute you, and say all manner of evil against you falsely, for My sake. Rejoice, and be exceeding glad, for great is your reward in heaven: for so persecuted they the prophets which were before you (Mt 5:3–4, 10–12).

Despite the fact that most of the slaves were illiterate, there were among them those who could read Holy Scripture, and thereby could pass along its teachings to their fellow bondsmen.

From the divinely inspired words, enslaved African Americans understood that every human being is made in the image of God. They knew that they were not meant to be slaves, and that they would, in time, be delivered from bondage.

In reading the Old Testament, the African American slaves identified with the Jewish people who were also under slavery. They knew how God delivered the Jews, and they had the same hope for themselves.

Their greatest hope, however, was in heaven. In the New Testament, they learned about deliverance not only from physical bondage (for example, the freeing of Sts. Peter and Paul from prison), but also from spiritual bondage, sin, death, and hell. Most crucially, they found that the way of overcoming these enemies of mankind was to be found in the divine-human Person of Jesus Christ who, by His commandments and continual presence in the lives of believers, leads His flock to His kingdom.

After the Emancipation Proclamation of 1863, white people in the South tried to hold onto whatever power they could over the former slaves. Thus, through segregation, black people still had to suffer in some form the indignities which they had endured under slavery, and of which the Lord had spoken: "Blessed are ye when men shall hate you, and when they shall separate you from their company, and shall reproach you, and cast out your name as evil for the Son of Man's sake" (Luke 6:22). At the same time, amid their hardships and afflictions they continued to find solace and joy in their experience of Christ's love.

African American Spirituals and Golden Age Gospel

SO FAR I'VE SPOKEN in a general way about the African American experience of Christ under slavery and then under Jim Crow. Now I'd like to speak about the songs through which they proclaimed that experience.

As I mentioned at the outset, the songs composed by African Americans under slavery came to be known as the Spirituals. These songs—expressing a profound awareness of the human condition as well as an ever-abiding hope in God —are of such transcendent beauty that they can arguably be considered America's greatest artistic achievement.

After the emancipation, African Americans continued singing their Spirituals at family gatherings and formal worship services; and they also performed them in countries overseas, where audiences were deeply moved by them. Of course, new songs were written during that time, which would be sung in the black churches as well. In time, these would come to be known as Gospel songs.

In the southern United States during the 1920s, black Gospel music developed a quartet style of *a cappella* singing. This decade saw the rise of such Gospel groups as the Swan Silvertones, the Soul Stirrers, and the Dixie Hummingbirds. A new creative infusion came in the 1930s, when the talented singer/songwriter Thomas Dorsey joined the Gospel ranks. Dorsey had been singing Gospel songs since the 1920s, but economic factors caused him to repeatedly return to writing and performing blues songs. Then, in 1932, in the wake of the sudden death of his wife and son during childbirth,

Dorsey turned the whole of his talent to Gospel music and left blues behind for good. The song he wrote in his grief over his family tragedy, "Precious Lord, Take My Hand," remains his best-known song.

The decade of the 1930s saw the further growth and expansion of the Gospel field, with the rise of such groups as the Roberta Martin Singers, of solo vocalists such as Mahalia Jackson, and of Gospel street singer/songwriters such as Blind Willie Johnson and Washington Phillips.

By this time, many of the Gospel groups and singers had begun to include musical instruments in their performances. The content and style—and especially the pathos—of black Gospel were inspired primarily by the Spirituals. However, there were other influences as well, notably from black secular music such as blues and jazz. Western classical music, which had been a source of inspiration in black churches of previous decades, continued to exert the same function, as can be heard in the vocals of such classically trained Gospel singers as Robert Anderson and Edna Gallmon Cooke.

As Gospel music was introduced into black churches, it elicited suspicion among some African American Christians, who thought it sounded too worldly. In time, however, the positive spiritual impact that Gospel music had on believers overrode this concern. While the musical style was varied, the content of the songs was purely Christian. The black Christians had a keen awareness of the difference between Gospel music, which glorifies God, and secular music, which glorifies sins and passions.

African American Gospel singers not only sang in churches; they also traveled throughout the United States and beyond, giving concerts along the way and thereby uplifting their people. In the era before Civil Rights, they were constrained by the fact that many venues did not allow blacks to perform there. Travel itself was a difficulty, because blacks could only stay in certain hotels and eat at certain restaurants. Nevertheless, traveling Gospel singers and groups became a major part of

African American culture. The term "Gospel Highway" was coined to describe the routes traveled by Gospel singers in order to spiritually feed their people while avoiding anti-black establishments. Sometimes there would be only one group on the program. At other times, several groups would perform at the same concert, giving their listeners an experience they would never forget. The burst of creativity that occurred during this period—creativity that was of the highest order in that it was dedicated solely to the Most High—has not been seen since, nor is it likely to occur again given the general decline in Christian Faith across the United States.

Some decades ago I was, like the African American church-goers mentioned earlier, at first suspicious of Gospel music, thinking it sounded too worldly. With a few exceptions, the only black Christian music I listened to was the Spirituals. Such purism, however, proved too limiting, since most of the early recordings of the Spirituals have Western classical settings. In time I decided to broaden the scope of my interest and give Gospel a chance. As I listened and re-listened to Gospel songs of the Golden Age, I was blown away. Like the Spirituals, they give voice to an undeniable experience of Jesus Christ, one that had been forged and sealed in suffering.

PATRISTIC THEMES

NOW THAT WE'VE EXAMINED how Christians throughout the ages—and African Americans in particular—have found a deeper connection with God through suffering, as well as how black Christians have described this connection in song, let's compare the writings of the Holy Fathers to the lyrics of Golden Age Gospel songs. The similarities are striking and not coincidental.

There are many spiritual themes in which one can find resonances between ancient Patristic writings and traditional black Gospel songs. Here we will restrict ourselves to four: (1) redemptive suffering (to which the reader has been introduced above); (2) the unavoidable reality that a true Christian is not at home in this world; (3) the fruits of the Spirit, which Christians experience when they take on redemptive suffering in devotion to Christ; and (4) the remembrance of death. We will begin with Patristic teachings, and then present comparable teachings in Golden Age black Gospel.

Redemptive Suffering

THE THEME OF REDEMPTIVE SUFFERING is so vast as to appear inexhaustible. In the history of the Church, no Life of a Saint has been written that has not had this theme front and center. The greatest heroes and heroines of the Church bore witness to the fact that the soul is closest to God when enduring afflictions with patience, devotion, and faith. It is then that we are as if lifted up above the earth. Our prayer becomes stronger when our hearts are broken. In our encounter with God amid suffering, we feel His presence and love, and we know that He alone is our hope and assurance. Our hearts become refined and purified as gold in the furnace, and we grow more in the divine likeness.

St. Thalassius of Libya, a Holy Father of the seventh century whose writings are found in *The Philokalia,* writes: "Fearful afflictions await the heart, for without great sufferings they cannot become pliable and responsive."[1]

Essentially, St. Thalassius is warning us against having hard hearts. With a hard heart, we make ourselves and those around us miserable, and we will not get into heaven. Therefore, the saint says, we have to make our hearts soft and pliable. We cannot do this without the help of our Lord Jesus Christ, for as He said we can do nothing without Him (cf. Jn 15:5). Therefore, in seeking to soften our hearts, we must cooperate with God. In the theology of the Orthodox Church, this is called "synergy," the working together of God and man.

In order to soften our hearts, God on His part sends us sufferings, but no more than we can bear (cf. 1 Cor 10:13). Our part is to repent of our sins, accepting the suffering while placing all our hope in Him.

If we do not repent, if we hold on to the hardness of our hearts, and do not take on voluntary sufferings for Christ's sake, God is going to give us afflictions in order to make our hearts soft. But there's good news: If God gives us sufferings in order to soften our hearts, that means He knows that we can change, that through trials and tribulations we can come closer to Him. On the other hand, if we experience no afflictions we should be concerned, because this may mean God knows our faith is so weak that if He sends us difficulties we will turn away from Him and become bitter.

Another Holy Father of the seventh century, St. Isaac the Syrian, wrote as follows on the spiritual value of suffering:

> The blessed Apostle [Paul] openly calls it a gift for someone to be ready in faith for suffering for the sake of his hope in God. Thus he says: *Unto you it hath been granted by God not only to believe in Christ, but also to suffer for His sake* (Phil 1:29). As St. Peter wrote in his epistle: *But and if ye suffer for righteousness' sake, happy are ye.... Rejoice, for ye are partakers of Christ's sufferings* (cf. 1 Pet 3:14, 4:13).
>
> Therefore, when you are at ease and enjoyment do not rejoice, and when tribulations come upon you do not be sullen or consider this as something alien to the way of God. For this path of God has been trodden from all the ages and through all generations by means of the Cross and death.
>
> Where do you get the idea that the afflictions on the path do not belong to the path? Do you not wish to follow in the footsteps of the saints? Do you want to travel by some special path of your own, one that does not involve suffering? The path to God is a daily cross. No one has ascended to God by way of ease. We know where the easy way leads![2]

In another place St. Isaac writes:

> Do not be astonished if, when you begin to practice virtue, severe tribulations break out against you on every side. Virtue is not counted virtue if it is not accompanied by

difficulty and by labors. That is why all those who … wish to live in Jesus Christ will suffer affliction. For He says: *If anyone will come after Me, let him deny himself, and take up his cross, and follow Me* (Mt 16:24).[3]

Through suffering we realize our infirmity and our need for God. Thus, the Holy Apostle Paul writes: "I take pleasure in infirmities, in reproaches, in necessities, in persecutions, in distresses for Christ's sake. For when I am weak, then am I strong" (2 Cor 12:10).

In fact, this is why God allowed suffering to enter the world in the first place. Our first ancestors, Adam and Eve, succumbed to the temptation of trying to become like God on their own. Suffering makes us realize that we're not God, and that we depend on Him for every moment of our existence. In other words, it dawns on us that we are really not so great after all, and that there is a God above us. That's when God comes and touches the soul. It is our preparation to dwell with Him forever in the kingdom of light and love.

Now I'll quote from *The Ladder of Divine Ascent* by St. John Climacus, a seventh century Holy Father who lived near Mount Sinai in Egypt. This is from Step 7 of *The Ladder*, "On Joy-making Mourning":

Mourning according to God is sadness of soul and the disposition of a sorrowing heart, which ever madly seeks that for which it thirsts; and when it fails in its quest, it painfully pursues it, and follows in its wake grievously lamenting. Or thus: mourning is a golden spur in a soul which is stripped of all attachment and of all ties, fixed by holy sorrow to watch over the heart.[4]

Here St. John is speaking of powerful, searing repentance. In Greek, the word for repentance is *"metanoia,"* which means literally to change the mind. Through *metanoia,* our minds are changed from the mind of this world of sinful passions into the mind of Christ.

Another passage, also from Step 7 of *The Ladder*, reads:

Groanings and sorrows cry to the Lord. Tears shed from fear intercede for us; but tears of all-holy love show us that our prayer has been accepted.[5]

When St. John speaks of tears shed from fear, he is referring to fear of punishment by God. Such tears are themselves a kind of prayer: thus the affirmation that they "intercede for us." Tears shed out of love for God, however, are an indication that He has brought compunction to a heart in order to soften it. This is a blessing in itself, but we should not grow proud of our tears or any other manifestation of grace, because the moment we become proud, the blessings disappear.

Christians Do Not Belong to This World

NOW LET'S TURN to another, related theme, namely, how we as Christians are not at home in this world. We have the words of our Lord on this topic:

> If the world hate you, ye know that it hated Me before it hated you. If ye were of the world, the world would love its own: but because ye are not of the world, but I have chosen you out of the world, therefore the world hateth you.... If they have persecuted Me, they will also persecute you (Jn 15:18–20).

This is what our Lord Jesus Christ foretold to His followers—and we've seen throughout the centuries that His words have proven true. The Christian Faith is at odds with the mind of this world, for the kingdom that our Lord preached is not of this world (cf. Jn 18:36).

According to Holy Fathers such as St. Isaac the Syrian and St. Ignatius Brianchaninov, the "world" in this context is not the world originally created good by God, but rather the world of sinful passions, ruled by the devil. The path of the Christian is arduous since he must counter this "world" both within and outside himself. St. Maximus the Confessor wrote about this in the seventh century:

Let us use peace in the right way. Repudiating our evil alliance with the world and its ruler, let us at last break off the war that we wage against God through the passions.... Nothing of profit will come to us from our peace in the world, for our soul is in an evil state, rebelling against its own Maker and unwilling to be subject to His Kingdom.[6]

When we speak of the Christian's arduous path, however, we must remember the promise of the Lord: that when we take upon ourselves His yoke and burden, we find them to be easy and light (cf. Mt 11:29–30). This is because Christ is with us in our suffering, caring for us, uplifting and healing our souls, burning off the dross of sin and leaving the precious gold of virtue.

The Fruits of the Spirit

THIS LEADS US to another commonality between the experience of the ancient Holy Fathers and African American Christians: the spiritual fruits derived from "changing one's mind" *(metanoia)* and giving oneself totally to Christ. The Holy Apostle Paul speaks of these as follows:

The fruits of the Spirit are love, joy, peace, longsuffering, gentleness, goodness, faith, meekness, temperance: against such there is no law. And they that are Christ's have crucified the flesh with the affections and lusts (Gal 5:22–24).

The highest of the virtues is the one that begins St. Paul's list: love. Christ said that love for God and one's neighbor is the greatest of the divine commandments (cf. Mt 22:37–40), and the Holy Apostles stressed its value in their epistles. St. John the Theologian wrote specifically about how Christians should strive for perfect love toward God and man (cf. 1 Jn 4:16–21). "Perfect love for God," he says, "casteth out fear." One who loves God in this way fears not punishment but only the possibility of losing one's Beloved. Perfect love for one's neighbor consists in loving everyone, since one cannot truly love God unless one loves all those made in His image.

71

St. Maximus the Confessor wrote two hundred short texts on love, which are found in the second volume of *The Philokalia*. Here he explains what perfect love for one's neighbor means:

> You have not yet acquired perfect love if your regard for people is still swayed by their characters. For example, if for some particular reason you love one person and hate another, or if for the same reason you sometimes love and sometimes hate the same person. Perfect love does not split up the single human nature, common to all, according to the diverse characteristics of individuals, but fixing attention always on this single nature, it loves all people equally.[7]

This, of course, is a tall order. There's no way that human beings could by their own power love everyone equally. It's only by the redemptive power of our Lord Jesus Christ—arising from His birth, life, death, resurrection, ascension, and sending down of the Holy Spirit—that His followers are even able to hope to attain such love.

In order to love in this manner, we must see our own sins and failings, realizing that, in common with the rest of the human race, we possess a nature that is good at its core but has been corrupted. If we know ourselves in this way, we can know others in the same way. We will not hate those who do evil, because we know there's something good in them; and we will not overly value people who seem to be good, because we know that even the greatest saints commit sins.

Remembrance of Death

THE FINAL PATRISTIC THEME we will explore is the remembrance of death. The Holy Fathers understood mindfulness of death to be an essential Christian practice. St. John Climacus writes in Step 6 of his *Ladder:* "As of all foods bread is the most essential, so the thought of death is the most necessary of all works." Speaking of the virtues arising from remembrance of death, he says that "these same virtues both produce the remembrance of death and are produced by it."[8]

As we know from the Scriptural/Patristic tradition of the Church, God allowed death into the world at the fall of Adam and Eve so that evil would not be immortal, and so that man would see the vanity of the sinful world that he himself had brought into being. Thus, for example, St. John Cassian wrote in the sixth century about how effective remembrance of death can be against the passion of avarice:

> We should remember how uncertain is the hour of our death, so that our Lord does not come unexpectedly and, finding our conscience soiled with avarice, say to us what God says to the rich man in the Gospel: *Thou fool, this night thy soul shall be required of thee: then who shall be the owner of what thou hast stored up?* (Lk 12:20).[9]

Mindfulness of death reminds us that we are limited creatures, with little time to live in this temporal world. If we view death with the eyes of faith, we can see even more: We can look beyond death to a continued existence in either heaven or hell, and to the resurrection of our bodies at the Last Judgment. St. Theodorus the Great Ascetic summarized this teaching in a treatise written for monastics:

> When sitting in your cell, do not act in a mindless and lazy manner.... Instead, work purposefully, concentrate your mind and always keep before your eyes the last hour before your death. Recall the vanity of the world, how deceptive it is, how sickly and worthless.... Recall the chastisements in hell, and the state of the souls imprisoned there. Recall, too, that great and fearful day, the day of the general resurrection, when we are brought before God, and the final sentence of the infallible Judge.... But think also of the blessings which await the righteous: how they will stand at Christ's right hand, the gracious voice of the Master, the inheritance of the Heavenly Kingdom, the gift which is beyond the mind's grasp, that sweet light, the endless joy....[10]

THE SAME THEMES
IN AFRICAN AMERICAN GOSPEL SONGS

AFTER EXAMINING some Scriptural/Patristic teachings that relate to the experience of African American Christians, we now come to the Golden Age Gospel songs that reflect these teachings.

Redemptive Suffering

WE'LL BEGIN WITH THE SONG "I Need the Lord to Guide Me" by The Trumpets of Joy of Aliquippa, Pennsylvania (Nashboro, 1961). This song is about redemptive suffering: about the narrow way of afflictions that we must travel as Christians. It is a beautiful expression of the Scriptural/Patristic teaching discussed earlier: that through suffering we realize our utter dependence on Jesus Christ. Our Savior and Lord is the only One Who can turn our afflictions into joy.

The song speaks of night vigils of prayer, in which the singer weeps before the Lord in desperation. It is not by accident that this practice mirrors that of Orthodox Christians (especially monastics) from ancient times until today, who have placed great value on night prayer, accompanied by tears, as a way to closer communion with Christ. The lyrics read:

> I need the Lord to guide me every day.
> Children, as I travel along this narrow way.
> Though afflictions oppress this soul of mine,
> I'm determined to reach my goal.
> I've got to have Jesus;
> I just can't make it by myself.
>
> Sometimes at night, I just have to walk the floor and cry;
> Sometimes, late in the midnight hour, I walk the floor
>   and cry;
> You know, I've got to have Jesus;
> I just can't make it by myself.
>
> Every time I feel this way,
> Lord, I pray every day for the light;
> Yes, I do.

You know, I pray and ask the Lord,
"Please don't leave me by myself!"

Every second, every minute, every hour of the day,
Through the weeks, through the months, through
    the years, come what may,
I've got to have Jesus;
I just can't make it by myself.

Sometimes at night, do you ever hang your head and cry?
Sometimes at night, I just hang my head and cry;
And then I need Jesus;
I just can't make it by myself.

Every time I feel this way,
I pray all night long,
Just like Daniel did when he was troubled.
You know, I pray and ask the Lord,
"Please don't leave me by myself."[11]

Christians Do Not Belong to This World

OUR NEXT SONG is by Dorothy Love Coates (1928–2002) and
her Singers (including her sister Lillian) of Birmingham, Alabama. Dorothy Love Coates not only sang the songs, she
wrote them as well—and not just a handful, but hundreds of
them. Most importantly (to borrow a phrase from a Thomas
Dorsey song), she lived the life she sang about: a life of faithfulness, virtue and sacrifice. For decades, her songs have been
sung in black churches all over the United States. Songs such
as "I've Got Jesus (and That's Enough)," "Ninety-Nine and a
Half Won't Do," "He May Not Come When You Want Him,
But He's Right on Time," and "You Must Be Born Again"
have helped to form the souls and shape the faith of new
generations of black American Christians.

The song we'll consider is called "The Old School," from
Dorothy's album *The Sound of Gospel* (Prestige, 1976). It's actually a suite of three songs interspersed with Dorothy's narration
about growing up in the black church. With an authenticity
born of nearly a half century of serving the Lord through thick

and thin, sunshine and rain, she tells us how black Americans of previous times found Christ in their afflictions. Both the songs and Dorothy's commentary touch on the theme of not being at home in this sinful world, which, as we've seen, has been a hallmark of genuine Christianity throughout the millennia. Here is the track transcribed in full:

Children, I'm from the Old School, namely the black church, where Gospel music originated many years ago and I was first introduced to the Gospel sound. The freedom and privileges we presently enjoy was not available to us back then; and being from a race who have suffered many years from financial depression, the old black minister couldn't afford an education, and the pianist who played the old upright piano in the corner wasn't musically educated. But the preaching, praying and singing that projected itself into the hearts and minds of my people kept hope alive in them. The black church was the school, and this was the sound:

> O Lord, You know
> I have no friend like You.
> If heaven's not my home,
> O Lord, what shall I do?
> The angels beckon me
> From heaven's open door,
> And I can't, I can't, I can't
> Feel at home in this world anymore.

My grandma and my grandpop used to say it like this:

> O Lord, You know
> I can't hear nobody pray.

They believed in prayer, and they felt that when folks stopped praying, the world was in a bad condition. See, they knew all about living in an unfriendly world. They had many trials and tribulations.

> And I can't, I can't, I can't
> Feel at home in this world anymore.

Long before they could afford an instrument, even the old upright piano that sat in the corner, they used to sing without music.* In this modern day and age, we call it *a cappella,* but they called it singing out of the soul. They used to keep the beat with the patting of the feet; they used to keep time by clapping their hands; they used to keep the rhythm with a bodily rock, as they swayed to and fro. And this is what the sound was like:

I'm just rolling.
I'm just rolling,
Lord, I'm just rolling
Through this unfriendly world.

Then they would start moaning. You see, moaning have a special significance, and it relates to my people. It's a way of communicating with God without doing it verbally. And the old folk used to say, "When you moan, Satan can't understand what you're talking about." They understood moaning, because they were a people of sorrow, well acquainted with grief.† They knew what it meant to want and not have, to need and not get, to feel misery and persecution and pain. And when you see 'em close their eyes and begin to rock and watch the tears roll down their face, they would say it one more time:

Lord, I'm just rolling
Through this unfriendly world.

You know, maybe that week somebody had stood in the courthouse and watched their son go to jail because they couldn't afford a lawyer. Maybe a father had gone out looking for a job, and couldn't find one. They had hopes and dreams like everybody else for the welfare and future of their children—but they say "I'm rolling through an unfriendly world."

---

* That is, without instrumental accompaniment.

† These words reflect what the Prophet Isaiah foretold about the Messiah that was to come: *He is despised and neglected of men: a man of sorrows, and acquainted with grief* (Is: 53:3). Dorothy applied this description to her own people, for just as Christ died on the Cross for our sake, so too are we called to bear our crosses for His sake.

The next song we'll examine is "I'm Looking for a Better Place to Live" by the Traveling Echoes of Louisville, Kentucky (Nashboro, 1956). As its title indicates, this song is also about Christians feeling not at home in this world and about their hope in heaven, where they can dwell in Christ, free from harm.

> Lord, I'm looking for a better place to live,
> Lord, after I die.
> Everyday I'm looking for a better place to live.
> Oh, yes, I am.
>
> Home don't seem like home
> In this old world anymore.
> Keep on looking for a better place to live.
>
> Ever since I've been leaning,
> Down here in this old world,
> This world of sin,
> I have trials and tribulations every day,
> Yes, I do.
> There's something more or less
> Always to destroy my happiness.
> Keep on looking.
> I've got to find me
> (Help me, Lord!);
> I've got to find me
> (O Lord!)—
> Find me a better place to live.

The Fruits of the Spirit

WE NOW TURN to the song "It's Jesus Y'all" by Troy Ramey and the Soul Searchers of Atlanta, Georgia (Nashboro, 1976). It concerns the fruits of God's grace bestowed on the soul that remains devoted to Him through all manner of difficulties. The lyrics are as follows:

> Something inside of me keep on bubblin' over.
> I got something inside of me, keep on bubblin' over.
> If anybody ask me I tell them:

"It's Jesus, y'all, I know it is."

Listen:
(Say it son!)
I got something inside of me, keep on holding the reins.
Something inside of me that I cannot explain.
If anybody ask me—
"It's Jesus, y'all, I know, I know, I know it is."
I'm not worried about it!
It's Jesus, y'all, I know it is.
Make you love everybody!
It's Jesus, y'all, I know it is.

I got something inside of me that I cannot explain.
Something inside of me make me cry when ain't nobody
botherin' me.
Let me tell you Who it is:
It's Jesus, y'all, I know it is.
Make me love everybody!
It's Jesus, y'all, I know it is.
Do you ever cry sometime in the midnight hour?
It's Jesus, y'all, I know it is.

Several fruits of the Spirit can be discerned in these lines. First, the singer speaks of the presence of Christ being inside of him and bubbling over: an image that Christ Himself used to describe the working of grace in His true servants (cf. Jn 4:14, 7:38). Secondly, he affirms that Christ "keeps on holding the reins" of his heart, that is, keeps it from giving in to sinful thoughts and feelings. Thirdly, he says that the presence of Christ within him makes him love everybody. This is clearly a visitation of God's grace, for, as noted above, it is impossible to love everybody except when God gives us the grace to do so.

In this light, I'd like to quote a brief but beautiful passage from an ex-slave. It was quoted in my article for *Foundations,* but it's so rich with meaning that it bears repeating here. In words recorded after the emancipation, the former slave speaks about the spiritual transformation that occurred in him through the power of Christ. He says:

I ran to an elm tree and tried to put my arms around it. Never had I felt such a love before. I just looked like I loved everything and everybody. The eyes of my mind were open, and I saw things as I never did before.[12]

The fourth spiritual fruit mentioned in the song "It's Jesus, Y'all" is the gift of tears. The singer observes: "Something inside of me make me cry when ain't nobody botherin' me." At such times, one weeps out of the sadness of repentance mingled with the joy of being aware of Christ's loving, forgiving presence. As will be recalled, St. John Climacus called this "joy-making mourning."

Remembrance of Death

TO COMPLETE THIS EXPLORATION of Golden Age Gospel, we'll look at songs concerning the remembrance of death. I've left this theme for last because I think it's the most remarkable. As we've seen, remembrance of death is one of the primary works of monks and nuns. St. John Climacus teaches that monastics living in stillness can undertake this work more effectively than people living in the world:

The remembrance of death among those in the midst of society gives birth to distress and ... even more to despondency; but among those who are free from noise it produces the putting aside of cares and constant prayer and the guarding of the mind.[13]

When one immerses oneself in Golden Age black Gospel, one finds that the theme of death comes up again and again: the death of family members (especially mothers) and friends, but most often one's own death. What I find remarkable about this is that the composers and singers of these songs were not monastics living in stillness, but "those living in the midst of society." Why did they not fall into despondency by constantly bringing to mind their own death? I believe it was because their hard conditions and harsh treatment by the dominant society gave them a more realistic perspective on what they rightfully called this "mean old sinful world," and thus a more sober-minded view of death.

We've seen how, during Gospel's Golden Age, singing groups traveled the Gospel Highway, giving concerts in churches and auditoriums. People would look forward to the next concert coming to their town or city, and they would pay an admission fee if it was held in a public venue. They would buy the albums, which they could draw inspiration from for the rest of their lives. From the viewpoint of our 21st century American society, which seeks to deny or hide the reality of death, and which relies on entertainment to *escape* from hard truths, it is amazing to think that these African American Christians *wanted* to be reminded of death in the Gospel songs they listened to. They paid hard-earned money to listen to songs with the message: "You're going to die. Prepare to meet your Maker."

A quintessential song on this theme, "Before This Time Another Year," speaks of the uncertainty of the hour of death, and also of the Christian's hope and joy beyond the grave. The song has seen many variations, including this poignant one sung by the Chosen Gospel Singers of Houston, Texas (Specialty, 1953):

> Before this time another year
> I may be dead and gone.
> In some lonesome graveyard:
> O Lord, how long?*
>
> Have mercy, Lord.
> I went in the valley,
> I went out there to pray.
> My soul got happy and I stayed all day.
> My body may be leaving,
> But my soul goes marching straight on home.
> Mother told me when I was young,
> Said a Christian's journey sometime get hard to run.

---

* The last two lines of this stanza have been added from a more common version of the song.

Gonna take Jesus for my guide,
For He'll stay right by my side.

While some Golden Age Gospel songs about death, like
the one above, express a longing for heaven, others warn of
God's judgment on unrepentant sinners. Such a warning can
be found, for example, in "God Almighty's Gonna Cut You
Down," a traditional song first recorded by the Golden Gate
Quartet of Norfolk, Virginia (Columbia, 1947):

You may run on for a long time,
Run on for a long time,
Run on for a long time:
Let me tell you, God Almighty's gonna cut you down.

Go tell that long-tongued liar,
Go tell that midnight rider,
Tell the gambler, rambler, backbiter,
Tell 'em God Almighty's gonna cut 'em down.

You may throw your rock and hide your hand,
Working in the dark against your fellow man.
But sure as God made the day and the night,
What you do in the dark will be brought to the light.
You may run and hide, slip and slide;
Tryin' to take the mote in your neighbor's eye.
But sure as God made rich and the poor,
You going to reap just what you sow.

You may run on for a long time,
Run on for a long time,
Run on for a long time:
Let me tell you, God Almighty's gonna cut you down.

Some people go to church just to signify.
Tryin' to make a date with the neighbor's wife.
But, Brother, let me tell you, sure as you're born,
You better leave that woman alone,
Because one of these days, mark my word,
You'll think that brother has gone to work.
You'll sneak up and knock on the door:
That's all, Brother, you'll knock no more.

Another song, "Get Away, Jordan" by Dorothy Love Coates and the Gospel Harmonettes (Specialty, 1951), does not shrink from portraying death in the starkest terms. It begins with words thought to have originated in an old Spiritual:

Get away, Jordan;
Get away, ole chilly Jordan:
I wanna cross over to see my Lord.

Then Dorothy sings in her own words:

I promised the Lord if He would set me free
I'd go to find out what the end might be.
One day, one day I was walking along.
I heard a voice but I saw no one.
The voice I heard sounded so sweet;
Came down from my head to the sole of my feet.
The friends that I used to love so dear:
They've gone on to glory and left me here.

When my feet get cold, my eyes are shut;
My body's been chilled by the hand of death;
Tongue glued to the roof of my mouth;
My hands folded across my breast.
You don't have to worry about how well I fare;
God Almighty He told me He'd be right there.

In one of her best-known songs, the aforementioned "Ninety-Nine and a Half Won't Do" (Specialty, 1956), Dorothy gave poetic expression to the words of our Lord: *He who endureth to the end shall be saved* (Mt 10:22). Dorothy sings:

I'm running, trying to make a hundred:
Ninety-nine and a half won't do.
It's a rugged, uphill journey, Jesus,
But I've got to make a hundred:
Ninety-nine and a half won't do.

The "hundred" that Dorothy refers to is not one hundred percent holiness, since we know from Scripture that only God is holy in the absolute sense (cf. Rev 15:4). Rather, our Lord expects from us something that is within our finite grasp: to never give up in the midst of trials and tribulations, but to remain with Him to the very end of our lives.

The song continues:

John the Baptist was a Forerunner of Christ.
They cut off his head and they took his life.
But when old death came riding on the headman's blade,
John looked up at him and smiled, because his hundred
    was made.
The head was exhibited on a platter in Rome,
But God took the soul from the body, and carried
    John home.

Ninety-nine and a half won't do.
Seventy, you won't make it;
Eighty, God won't take it;
Ninety, that's close;
Ninety-nine and a half is almost.
But get your hundred:
Ninety-nine and a half won't do.

FINALLY, AS WE CONCLUDE this comparison of ancient Patristic wisdom and Golden Age black Gospel, let us take to heart their common message. Let us resolve to suffer all things for Christ's sake, believing that He is working all things for good in order to purify and perfect us (see Rom 8:28). With humility, forgiveness, and longsuffering, may we ascend toward the height of perfect love for God and man. There we will catch a glimpse of the future age that God has prepared for His true servants, where love will reign supreme and Christ will be all in all.

5

DOROTHY LOVE COATES

AND THE AFRICAN AMERICAN SPIRITUAL TRADITION

FR. DEACON JOHN GRESHAM

I WANT TO THANK Abbot Damascene Christensen and Hieromonk Herman Grace not only for preserving but also for passing down the legacy of Dorothy Love Coates. By doing this, they have shared an example of the religious music I grew up with in the rural African American black church tradition.

In his presentation for the Fellowship of St. Moses the Black, Abbot Damascene noted the "Golden Age" of African American Spirituals to be between the 1940s and the 1960s, with some performers being active into the '80s and '90s. The extension of that era was alive and well in communities outside of the major cities. Churches in Baltimore, Washington DC, and even Richmond, introduced more contemporary sounds and instrumental arrangements in their music as early as the 1970s. Saints* in my grandparents' generation in places like King William, Tappahanock and Warsaw, Virginia weren't "up to speed" in part because there weren't

---

* Righteous church-goers.

enough younger church members to bring such styles to the country churches. Many blacks of my parents' generation were seeking greener pastures in metropolitan areas. Also, the older folks in the 1970s and '80s didn't like "bumpity bumpity" music in the church.

I confess that I don't recall Dorothy Love Coates and her group by name, although I probably heard her music on the Gospel radio programs my parents and grandparents played every Sunday morning. The names of spiritual singing groups were fairly similar. The name of the Original Harmonettes sounds about as common as Maggie Ingram and the Ingramettes (a popular group during my childhood), the Jackson Southernaires, Gospel Tones, Swan Silvertones, Staple Singers, Harvey Singers (another local group). Even in my years as a Baptist pastor in rural King William County, there were always a few singing groups that would be invited to put on or be a part of a program for Mother's Day, the Church Anniversary, or some other occasion. Many congregations are made up of elderly men and women who grew up on the Spirituals. I was a part of a county-wide choir that sang the older Negro Spirituals and songs from the decades before the "Golden Age" began. The music was still quite popular in black country churches, probably up until COVID-19 restrictions kept most worshipers home.

I feel comfortable referring to her as "Sister" or "Mother" Dorothy because that's how we addressed Gospel artists when they came to perform and worship with us. They would never play before a "watching and waiting" audience when they came to, say, New Second Little Elam Baptist Church.* A few people, if not the entire congregation, would get up singing and clapping along with the group. Somebody "gettin' happy" was an expectation, even among non-Pentecostal churches. If Sister Dorothy and the Harmonettes stepped foot in one of the churches of my childhood, they would be a part of a larger, shared experience.

---

* A fictitious name based on reality.

The shared experience between Sister Dorothy and my community was of faithful struggle. African Americans in Alabama bore the same insults and injustices as those in Virginia and anywhere else in Jim Crow America (parts of the Midwest were no better than the South). We all altered Spirituals and made up "freedom songs" as we marched and protested during the Civil Rights Movement. A student from West Point, Mississippi would need to rely on familial bonds with local blacks in Newport News as he attended Hampton Institute. Local churches looked out for soldiers from other parts of the country stationed at Fort Bragg in North Carolina or Fort Hood in Texas (both bases named for inept Confederate generals). This persecution was very similar to that of early Christians who faced torture and death by the Romans no matter what part of the empire they were from or what they looked like. Orthodox Christians under Islamic and communist regimes also had to bond with each other out of necessity. Suffering brought people together for the sake of survival.

In that struggle, great faith was born and people saw it in each other. In one story about her, someone described Sister Dorothy as a preacher. While there were always false prophets in every culture and situation, African American Christians of that era had a sense of seeing godliness in each other. Even if a singer didn't have great talent, if she spoke wisely from the Scriptures or was known for encouraging young people to do well in school or a trade, she would be invited back to sing based on her Christian character. This isn't very different from the monastic communities of Africa and the Middle East where a greatly known man like Abba Arsenios would confess his thoughts to an unnamed monk of native Egyptian peasant stock. "I know Greek and Latin. But I don't know this man's alphabet."[1] Arsenios saw a holy wisdom in that monk that he could learn from. As they say among modern-day street hustlers, "game knows game."

In her version of "(You Can't Hurry God) He's Right on Time," Sister Dorothy said that Job lost his wife, as he did his children and everything else he had. To be biblically accurate, Job's wife was still alive. She did not have the same faithfulness to God in this time of distress. Therefore, she was, in a way, lost. In another song,* she sings that the head of John the Baptist was presented on a platter in Rome. Again, the scriptures indicate Jerusalem. Four hundred years later, his head was sent to Constantinople, the new Rome. What mattered most to African American Spirituals was not the biblical accuracy, but the undeniable message of salvific truth in the lyrics. God could not be hurried. This was a truth that any African American knew as the people experienced Him. The status of Job's wife was a minor point. John the Baptist lived in full righteousness before God, and we are called to strive to live likewise no matter what the cost. "Ninety-nine and a Half Won't Do." Pastors could make whatever corrections necessary in a sermon or Sunday school lesson. The job of the singer was to proclaim the truth.

The traditional black Spirituals sung by Dorothy Love Coates and others like her were born out of a Christian community of shared struggle, fellowship, and hope. These three elements bound African American Christians (and non-Christians) together even in my generation. I grew up attending integrated schools from kindergarten. I saw the repercussions of the bussing issue in the metro Richmond area and white flight in a Henrico County neighborhood. In my community, we had intact black families from a variety of surrounding counties and occupations. When not going to our church in King William (we had services twice a month with a pastor who had two churches), we frequently attended services in town with family friends from Charles City County who joined a congregation nearby. As kids, we would all attend each other's Vacation Bible School during the summer. The music was the lifeblood of our worship as we had most songs and styles in common. Sister Dorothy would have been another beloved mother of my childhood. May her memory be held eternally.

---

* For the lyrics, see Abbot Damascene Christensen's article, p. 84.

6

THE
LITURGY
IS A WAR CRY
HOMILY
TO THE CHOIR

FR. TURBO QUALLS

T HE DIVINE LITURGY is the connection between those in heaven and those on earth. This is a reality which we need to grasp more deeply. All of our work for social improvement will be for naught if we don't know that the Liturgy is both our weapon and our war cry. In the Book of Revelation, St. John pulls back the veil to the "holy and celestial and mystical altar"* where the heavenly Liturgy takes place. With this vision as our starting point, we want to move towards understanding the correspondence between the heavenly and the earthly.

> When he had opened the fifth seal, I saw under the altar the souls of them that were slain for the word of God, and for the testimony which they held: And they cried with a loud voice, saying: How long, O Lord, holy and true, dost thou not judge and avenge our blood on them that dwell on the earth? And white robes were given unto every one

---

* From the Divine Liturgy of St. John Chrysostom.

of them; and it was said unto them, that they should rest yet for a little season, until their fellow servants also and their brethren, that should be killed as they were, should be fulfilled (Rev 6:9–11).

St. John is speaking of the martyrs—the martyrs in heaven who are numbered and are awaiting God's judgment. They are awaiting God's reconciliation, His justice. I might also venture to say that St. John is speaking of us, too. That is because we are on earth awaiting that same judgment, and interceding for this world. The Liturgy is the place of intercession. Let's look at what St. Paul says in his first epistle to Timothy.

I exhort therefore, that, first of all, supplications, prayers, intercessions, and giving of thanks, be made for all men; for kings, and for all that are in authority; that we may lead a quiet and peaceable life in all godliness and honesty. For this is good and acceptable in the sight of God our Savior; Who will have all men to be saved, and to come unto the knowledge of the truth. For there is one God, and one mediator between God and men, the man Christ Jesus; Who gave himself a ransom for all, to be testified in due time (1 Tim 2:1–6).

These prayers, these petitions, and these intercessions that we offer, they're especially necessary when the rulers and governments of this world are making choices based on the values of this world, and not the values of the heavenly kingdom. These prayers are especially needed when rulers are guided by their passions rather than trying to overcome their passions—this is when the prayers of Christians for their rulers are particularly important. The hallmark of Christians is not that we pray for people who enact the policies that we want. It is, instead, that we pray with compassion, even for those who are doing evil in the world. That's the example Christ and the saints set for us. St. Silouan says that if you can't pray for enemies, the grace of God is not with you.

The Liturgy is the place where we ask God to have mercy on the world. We, as Christians, have been tasked to do this work. That's part of what it means to be His chosen people. We are chosen to be the bridge between the loving God and the sinful world which He loves. The main thing I want to get across here is what we referenced above, there is one God, and one Mediator between God and men, the man Christ Jesus. The name of Jesus is above all names. That is the secret. But the problem is that we have all been saturated with the misuse of the name of Jesus. Jesus doesn't mean anything to society anymore because everyone's already been a Christian of some sort and then moved on to something else. People see the name of Jesus on TV spoken without reverence. People hear the name of Jesus taken in vain. And there's a reason for that. There's a reason nobody ever says, "Oh Buddha!" when they are upset. No one does that because the name of Buddha hasn't been diluted to meaningless syllables. It is Christianity that has been watered down in this way. In making common of the name of Christ, the power is taken away. So, it's important for us to understand and remember that the name of Jesus is powerful, and to reclaim that power.

The Wisdom of God, is Jesus Himself. He is what we are proclaiming and how we are achieving everything. When we intercede for misguided governments, or evil happening in the world, we need to see that there is a spiritual world operating behind what we see. Let me give an example. In big business, profits are made by catering to the fallen human passions—greed, sexuality, violence in particular. When a spirit of greed infuses a business, they will do anything to make money, exploiting both workers and the public. And if you change the CEO or board members, is this passionate spirit going to dissipate? No. Then where does this spirit come from? This is where we get deeper into it. This isn't based on some modern, progressive theology, but on how our forefathers saw the world. Our forefathers of the Church saw the world with eyes free from secular materialism. They understood that the spiritual realm penetrates and guides the visible world.

Now, when you hear of principalities, powers and spiritual warfare, you have to stop thinking about winged ninjas battling with swords in the sky—never mind that it's a cool image. And you have to stop thinking about the little purple demon on your shoulder saying, "Eat that chocolate." We need to enlarge our thinking. There is a real spiritual battle happening all around us which we are blind to. The powers of light and the powers of darkness are engaged in a battle for each human soul.

The Liturgy is a war cry for those of us who want to fight on the side of the powers of light, with God's holy angels. There is a reason why the Liturgy is served frequently, or even daily, in many places. That is because it's the most effective weapon we have in this fight. As an individual, there's not much you can do about the gun violence in your neighborhood. There's little you can really do about human trafficking happening all around you. There's not much that you can do to solve the injustices that you see amongst your brothers in the neighborhood. But there is something that we actually can do effectively. We can receive heavenly wisdom. And that wisdom can help us make the change where it really matters.

When we deepen our Orthodox worldview—because this is what we have been talking about—when we deepen it and this informs our prayer, and our prayer informs our action, then meaningful change begins to happen. Because if we set out to fix the world on our own strength, based upon our feelings of morality, we are still motivated by human passions, just like the big business I mentioned above. This is where most protest movements go wrong— "I'm offended by something, so I'm going to do x, y, and z." It's battling passion with passion—just moving shells around, as I like to say. You may stop one little thing right in front of you. But the spirituality which motivated that thing hasn't been touched. That is the one area where at times the Civil Rights movement actually was powerful. People forget that these were Christian movements and they weren't just dependent on good organization. There was a spiritual force channeled into disciplined action. The nonviolence with which they were able to endure was because they were spiritually rooted and formed. That's why the social justice movements of today don't have the same power. They have rage, anger, and indignation, but there's no real power to change because they are not spiritual movements. They are moralistic; they're just moving shells around again. They have moved the wall of enmity but they have not removed it.

The early Church understood this quite clearly. When the Roman magistrates ordered the early Christians to worship false gods for the support of the empire, they refused. Instead, as their support of the empire, they chose to kneel and offer prayers to God on the emperor's behalf. You know the frequent story of the early martyr. What happens? The governor says, "You must throw incense to the idol!" Now, you might say to yourself, "What's the big deal? It's just incense." But do you think any of the martyrs thought, "What's the big deal? Just go throw some incense and you can go." Why wouldn't they do that? Was it the incense? No. An offering of incense was the completion of the spiritual reality, and they understood that. There is a spiritual force behind that idol which they would be aligning themselves with if they threw that incense. This seemingly innocuous act was a far more serious denial of their beliefs than we might think today.

Pay attention here. A movement of rebellion, in this case, would simply acknowledge the absolute and ultimate seat of the emperor's power, and then attempt to seize it. All rebellion does, basically, is to say, "Yeah, you are the big man. You've got the power and I want it." So, it perpetuates the cycle of tyranny. That's why those who overthrow tyrants normally become tyrants themselves, because they never address the spirituality. They're just swapping bodies. Moving the same shells around to their own liking. The devil is fine with your raging about injustice, because as long as you're raging it's just fueling the same fire. Rebellion focuses solely on the physical institution and its current incumbents and attempts to displace them by an act of superior force. It says, "I don't like the way you treat me so I'm going to get back at you. And then, when I'm king, I'm going to treat you just as brutally as you treated me." In the end, nothing has changed.

Prayer denies that passionate spirit altogether, by acknowledging the higher power of the Godhead, making physical rebellion unnecessary. Prayer cuts it off at the knees instead of playing into the same game that the devil plays. The prayers of the martyrs challenged the very spirituality of the empire, and called the empire's angel—the spirituality of the empire, as it were—before the judgment seat of God. This is the thing to understand about intercession and spiritual warfare. It isn't just lawmakers and boards who make decisions. It's not just the president or CEO shaping policy. See, that's where many of us have it twisted. It's also these principalities that motivate them and move them.

For us modern Christians, we've lost the sense of this. It's a necessary part of our warfare! For so many Christians, Sunday service means you come in and you fulfill your religious obligation. Or you come in and feel better. We sing some songs and we're together. Isn't that sweet? But that's not the fullness of why we're here. That's not what the Liturgy is ultimately for. That's not how our spiritual forefathers engaged the Liturgy. For them, and for the martyrs, the Liturgy was the way to counteract the principalities of darkness and bring in the heavenly reign. We must learn to address the spiritual forces as well as their visible manifestations with this: the name and the power of Jesus Christ.

I can go out there and adopt this cool "Fr. Turbo" persona on the street. I can try to get people to rally behind me and get some kind of movement done. But it doesn't really change the world. It's not going to shift anything on the spiritual plane. Real shifts begin first with us, inside us. Then it will happen that someone will encounter you on the street and, over a simple conversation, will be profoundly touched by something you said because they heard Christ speaking through you. They are changed by that glimpse of Christ. These are the ways that you begin to actually make a shift in the world's spirituality; but you can't do it unless you totally imbibe the true spirituality yourself.

Understand what we're doing in our churches in the Liturgy. It starts right there with each of you, as you let go of the idea that you're just coming in and checking your religious obligation. You're not just singing songs. Angels are with us. Angels are with us and things begin to move and to change. This is not done on our strength. This is on the strength of Christ our God.

I want to close this loop on how the material and spiritual realities affect each other, so think about this: Have you ever tried to find a valid reason why they killed Jesus? I encourage you to do that—actually, go search the Gospels. Why did they kill Jesus? He challenged their authority. Is that it? But whose authority was it that He challenged? He challenged the authorities of this world and the principalities behind them and they could not tolerate it. So, they had Him executed. It was not a mistake. He was a holy terror to the spirits of darkness. He had to be removed because He undoes the kingdom of this world. In regards to politics and worldly authority, Christ chose to be powerless; yet, in the midst of His voluntary powerlessness He still had all the ultimate power of the Godhead. He comes in meekness and says, "My kingdom is not of this world" (Jn 18:36). That's why when James and John come and say, "Give us the word, and we'll call down fire from heaven on these Samaritans!" Jesus responds, "You don't know what spirit you are of; if I want to, I can call down twelve legions of angels in my defense" (cf. Lk 9:54–56 & Mt 26:53). His power is something different. God is love. That love is not saccharine; it does powerful things. It's the power to forgive enemies. That's true power.

God, in His voluntary powerlessness before the free will of man, lays man low. When man is laid low he is able to repent, his heart is softened and he begins to be malleable in the hands of God. To remember Jesus is the key. We have to rise above the saturated misconception of Jesus Christ. We need to get at who He really is, at His power. St. Sophrony of Essex will help us out here, go ahead and read this slowly:

> The liturgy in its eternal reality is the Lord's Passover permanently present with us. Before the coming of Christ, the Jewish Passover commemorated the historical event of the crossing of the Red Sea. But our Passover is Christ and He bids us to commemorate His name: This do in remembrance of me. Thus, He, the true center of the universe and not simply some historical event, is the focus of our attention. Our Passover, and therefore also our Eucharist, is a passage from earth to heaven, from death and sin to the holy eternity of the Father. Taking part as fully as possible in the liturgical act gradually teaches the faithful to participate in Christ's Gethsemane prayer.[1]

This is essentially what the Liturgy is. We are not simply reminiscing about something, saying, "Oh, do you remember we went on that vacation?" It's a different thing than a sentimental recollection. It's actually being present at what we commemorate, partaking in that reality. When the Jews celebrated the Passover, they didn't just entertain themselves with fables about Moses. They were there again; they were experiencing the escape from Egypt. And when we perform the Eucharist in remembrance of Christ, we are truly present with Him at the Last Supper. Now, back to St. Sophrony and the Gethsemane prayer:

> This is the pattern when we are pierced by sorrow, pain, loss. We transfer our own hurt to the universal plane and suffer not merely for ourselves but for all humanity. To the extent of our personal experience, we can live every man's tragic lot. His dread and his despair. It may be that our suffering will at some point exceed our powers of endurance. Then, when mind and body can no longer keep up with the spirit, the spirit continues to follow after Christ to the crucifixion, to the grave, into the anguished hell of his love for mankind.[2]

This is what happens when we are in the Liturgy. Let's connect what we are saying to something specific. When the priest lifts up the paten* and the chalice and says, "Thine own of Thine own," you can put on that paten your pain. Put on the paten the brokenness of your grandfather. Put on the paten your friend who lost her child. This is the connection between our suffering and Christ's, between the earthly and the heavenly. And when we say, "Again and again in peace, let us pray to the Lord," what is that? It's a supplication. What are we doing? We're asking God for mercy, and not just for ourselves but for all mankind past, present, and future. That mercy is what we all need. When people come to church, they are coming for hope. They're coming for a reprieve. They're coming for healing. They're coming for divine direction.

In this world, which is where we're all called to be, many people are so grief-stricken, they don't even know how to call out anymore. So, we must call out for them. When we say, "Lord have mercy," it's not a little thing. We need to sorrow with "every man's tragic lot." People need to be free to bring their sorrow, and their brokenness, and their trauma into our church. That's why we're here. That's the purpose of the Liturgy—healing, transformation, and union with God.

Now, let's look for the fulfillment of this principle in the prophecy of Isaiah:

> He was despised and forsaken of men, a man of sorrows and acquainted with grief; and like one from whom men hide their face He was despised, and we did not esteem Him. Surely our griefs He Himself bore, and our sorrows He carried; yet we ourselves esteemed Him stricken, smitten of God, and afflicted. But He was pierced through for our transgressions, He was crushed for our iniquities; the chastening for our well-being fell upon Him, and by His scourging we are healed. All of us like sheep have gone

---

* Also called "diskos," the paten is a small golden plate on a stand which holds the "Lamb"—the piece of bread which will be consecrated into the Body of Christ during the Liturgy.

astray, each of us has turned to his own way; but the Lord has caused the iniquity of us all to fall on Him (Is 53:3–6).

That is the Gethsemane prayer that we are endeavoring to join Christ in, bearing the pain and iniquities of all people on our shoulders in the Liturgy. That is the kind of prayer which sends light to everyone out there in pain, in the ghettos, in darkness. That's what's going on in the Divine Liturgy. You see, we're begging God for mercy, and we're trying to do the real work of healing the world from its spiritual darkness.

Here is a suggestion. I encourage you to start listening to some Negro Spirituals. Not Gospel music—except, perhaps, from the Golden Age of Gospel, like Dorothy Love Coates*—but old time Negro Spirituals. You're going to find something. There is this uncanny touchpoint between the Spirituals and ancient liturgical music—not the choral stuff of now. I mean the ancient Orthodox liturgical music—like Byzantine or Znamenny. You will find in that music bright sorrow. There is always, without a hint of despair, a seasoning of pain and sorrow. Why is this? Because our Orthodox forefathers knew that this wasn't their home, and the Negro slaves did also. They both understood that this world is not our true home; the Kingdom of Heaven is. Whether under the emperor or the slave master, this world is not the end goal. The Liturgy is where people can experience the other world, their true home.

I hope visitors can enter an Orthodox service for the first time and be stopped in their tracks. Not just because it's a different world culture than what they know. I want to see them engage the Liturgy and be struck by the presence and the power of prayer. A prayer which carries all the pain of the world on its shoulders. Sorrow, not sorrow as the world sorrows but godly sorrow, is something to be desired (cf. 2 Cor 7:10). We are joining Christ in His Gethsemane prayer, heading for the Cross and the Resurrection.

---

* See Dn. John Gresham's article, p. 85.

That's why Great Lent is so powerful. Who could not mourn when we begin the Lamentations on the night of Holy Friday? Then we have Psalm 50, the most commonly used psalm in the divine services telling us, "A broken and contrite heart God will not despise." It is better to be in the house of mourning than the house of mirth (cf. Ecc 7:4). This is not about being morose. This is not about being Eeyore, down in the dumps. This is the key to real joy. This is the difference between happiness and joy. I don't care about your worldly happiness. God sets His sights beyond our worldly happiness because it is associated with temporality. "I'm happy because I have an iPhone ... because I'm going to have shepherd's pie ... because I have a Frappuccino." How is it that Africans have joy? What is it? It's the suffering. It's not morose self-pity—that's not suffering. People who really suffer, they don't fall into self-pity. Self-pity is for those who are complacent and unwilling to suffer. Let me leave off with a look at the eternal, Divine Services in Revelation:

I beheld, and, lo, in the midst of the throne and of the four beasts, and in the midst of the elders, stood a Lamb as it had been slain, having seven horns and seven eyes, which are the seven Spirits of God sent forth into all the earth. And he came and took the book out of the right hand of him that sat upon the throne. And when he had taken the book, the four beasts and four and twenty elders fell down before the Lamb, having every one of them harps, and golden vials full of odors, which are the prayers of saints. And they sung a new song, saying, Thou art worthy to take the book, and to open the seals thereof: for thou wast slain, and hast redeemed us to God by thy blood out of every kindred, and tongue, and people, and nation; and hast made us unto our God kings and priests: and we shall reign on the earth. And I beheld, and I heard the voice of many angels round about the throne and the beasts and the elders: and the number of them was ten thousand times ten thousand, and thousands of thousands; saying with a loud voice, Worthy is the Lamb that was slain to receive power, and riches, and wisdom, and strength, and honor, and glory, and blessing. And every creature which is in heaven, and on the earth, and under the earth, and such as are in the sea, and all that are in them, heard I saying, Blessing, and honor, and glory, and power, be unto him that sitteth upon the throne, and unto the Lamb for ever and ever. And the four beasts said, Amen. And the four and twenty elders fell down and worshipped him that liveth for ever and ever (Rev 5:6–14).

The four creatures are traditionally interpreted to be the four Evangelists, but we could also see them as the four corners of the earth. The twenty-four elders are the twelve tribes of Israel and the twelve apostles. Here's another angle—the icon of Pentecost has an old man sitting at the bottom. He is Cosmos, the world. He's holding this little satchel and it has twelve scrolls: the teachings of the twelve apostles who enlightened him, i.e., the entire universe. All of the world worships the Lord Jesus Christ, and every knee will bow and every tongue will confess Him. That is our war cry. And that's why we say "Blessed is the kingdom of the Father and the Son and Holy Spirit" to begin the Divine Liturgy. It isn't all happy and nice and neat. It is war. Human trafficking, gun violence, racism, sexism, oppression—all of that … nothing can stand against Him because He will make everything right. And we of all people must know this. We must hold the front line until He comes again.

So, when you come and sing, don't just come in and punch your timecard. This isn't a barbershop quartet. This is war. Don't bury your sorrows and feel like you need to look good and be all put together at church. Bring your sorrows to the Liturgy. Bring your frustrations to the Liturgy. Bring the world's sorrows to the Liturgy. That's what is going to get you to really sing. That's what will bring into the choir true, soulful prayer. That's what will season your voices with the sound of bright sadness which is the signature of the heart of Orthodox worship.

II
MUSICALITY

7

AMERICAN ORTHODOX MUSIC

TOWARDS A SYNTHESIS

HIEROMONK ANDREW WERMUTH

F ROM THE MISTS OF TIME, music has been integral to the human worship of God. So often, it has provided the form through which people expressed the content of their prayer to God. Perhaps the foremost example is that of the holy Prophet David, who wrote his prayers in poetic form to be sung and accompanied by the twelve-stringed psaltery. In reading the Psalms, we sense that it is the poetic and musical qualities of these prayers that raise the heart to express its inner recesses. The early Christian Church adopted St. David's mode of prayer not only in reciting the psalms composed by him, but by lifting up the Church's prayer to God in song.

Throughout its life, the Church has witnessed various types of liturgical music in different ages and locales. And while these modes have varied greatly, there has remained a foundation which will never be shaken in any Orthodox liturgical music. That foundation is the ethos of St. David's psalms. This ethos centers on the glorification of God's goodness and power, and the appeal of a contrite heart for His mercy. This overarching factor, together with many more specific elements, should be kept in mind when Orthodox Christians in America consider the future of their liturgical music.

In examining these elements, I will discuss the work of several current leaders in the realm of Orthodox liturgical music in America. While this survey is no way exhaustive, it should open the topic of what Church musicians must consider when composing or adapting* liturgical music for America. These observations will inevitably lead to a reflection on the American identity and its cultural heritage, and a consideration of how this relates to the work of creating liturgical music in this country.

Elements of Liturgical Music

IN AMERICA TODAY, one of the foremost figures in Orthodox music is the accomplished choir director, composer, opera conductor, musicologist, and writer Mark Bailey. He studied at the Yale Institute of Sacred Music, and taught at St. Vladimir's Seminary. Several of his original liturgical compositions are used by parishes and monasteries in the OCA.

In one of his articles he offers a defining characteristic of Church music: "music becomes liturgical only when it clearly communicates sacred text and accurately brings into existence the ceremonial component to which it is assigned."[1] That is, the music is dictated by the content and context of the prayer. "Any other point of view inevitably factors in personal tastes," says Bailey.[2] The Church Fathers and the prayers of the Church remind us that liturgical prayer is always "rational." While the beauty of liturgical music may reach unearthly heights, it is never divorced from the Word which it proclaims.

---

* "Adapting" a translated liturgical hymn means adjusting the translation or the melody, or both, so that the music optimally expresses the prayer in the new language.

Bailey also suggests that a Church musician should be aware of the history of liturgical music. An example he gives is that

> the presence and role of psalm texts in pristine liturgy led to the development of verse-refrain structure as the means by which antiphons were set musically. Knowledge like this reinforces that musicians should never detach liturgical music from its ceremonial purpose, by which one may determine its primary qualities without compromising the integrity of rite.[3]

Historical Models

USING HISTORY to investigate the process of the synthesis of liturgical music, we can look back to the conversion of the Slavs. In becoming Orthodox, the Russians, Bulgarians, Macedonians, and Serbs took the already highly developed form of Byzantine music and gradually personalized it through the addition of favorite indigenous musical phrases or *popevki*. A similar occurrence happened when the Russian Church evangelized the natives of Alaska. A slight variation in the Russian melodies resulted in the "Alaska Tones."

These examples provide evidence that it is legitimate for a newly Orthodox people to flavor their liturgical art in a personal way, as long as the basic ethos of the chant remains in the spirit of David. In this sense, "personal" can be understood as something that reflects the identity of a particular people rather than the "personal" taste of an individual composer.

Bailey also claims that "it is legitimate for current culture to desire degrees of expression in worship."[4] He tells us that previous generations "drew on the best of culture, to ensure that they would express beautifully and at the highest level known to them. This of course explains the unavoidable similarities between Byzantine liturgy and Byzantine high culture."[5] With this thesis he continues on to justify the 18th century westernizing influences on Church music that occurred under the "high culture of Catherine the Great"— a development that became known as the St. Petersburg

School. He also says that those who did not accept homophonic chant* and held to unison chant became sectarians
("Old Believers"). While others might ask whether the St. Petersburg School had not to some degree distorted the essential Orthodox ethos, it nevertheless brings one to ponder our
present circumstances and raises the question, "What is the
best of American culture?"

Until We Sing and Dance

IN AN ONLINE ARTICLE entitled "Mission and Worship—America and the Orthodox," Fr. Stephen Freeman† presents St.
Paul's mandate to "be all things to all men" (1 Cor 9:19–23)
as the basis for the Church's mission in America. On the topic
of inculturation, he makes the following disclaimer: "we
should not confuse American culture with the music, etc.,
being marketed by mass media to various niche groups. ...
This is mass culture—produced and marketed to people's
passions to exploit in many cases the very lowest element of
their nature. As such, this should not be considered culture."[6]

As Christians we view society with a hierarchy of values
based on the Gospel teaching. Not everything is of equal value.
In the consideration of adapting music from an existing culture into liturgical music, inevitably the question arises: How
can this be done without compromising the Orthodox ethos?

Before their Christianization, the Slavs possessed a rich
cultural life. When they became Orthodox, feast days were
celebrated in liturgical worship followed by common gatherings in which traditional foods were served and music was
celebrated in the form of song and dance. But, according to
the consensus of American Orthodox, we no longer sing and
dance. When Fr. Stephen adds, "There's something wrong

---

* "Homophonic chant" is harmonized in a simple manner such that all the
parts follow the rhythm of the lead part.
† The V. Rev. Stephen Freeman is retired from his positions as Dean of the
South in the OCA and pastor of St. Anne's Orthodox Church in Oak
Ridge, Tennessee.

with a nation where people don't sing and dance," he speaks for many. One commentator even speculated, "And until we sing and dance, our liturgical music will remain synthetic"— "synthetic" in the sense of two things coming together yet remaining essentially two separate things (as opposed to two things being joined and becoming ontologically one).

Many of us would agree that he has a point. This connects with Mark Bailey's claim that it is legitimate for a country's national music to color its liturgical music. However, the gap is to be found in the apparent lack of true culture in present day America. And if cultural life, being a reflection of a nation's spiritual life, has reached a low ebb, how can such a nation create a legitimate liturgical music? Does America really lack any genuine culture altogether? Is postmodern consumerism the only ethos that we have to relate to today?

American Roots and Culture

ACCORDING TO FOLKLORISTS and musicologists there is indeed great value to be found in American culture. Two leaders in the study of American folklore in the 20th century were John and Alan Lomax. This father and son team toured the country collecting folk songs for three years in the 1940s. Both were astute scholars and musicians. As such they absorbed the American musical tradition in a personal way—by playing and listening to music in the homes of their fellow countrymen. Many of these unique sessions were recorded and are now preserved in the Library of Congress archives. Alan Lomax describes America's music as follows:

> Out of the tune-stock that poured from the British Isles and out of the heritage of rhythms and song-styles welling up in the hearts of the African slaves, a deep river of song was formed that has coursed through the lives of all Americans. A deep river of melody and profoundest emotion that washed the pain and sorrow from the souls of millions pioneering who made America strong and free. A deep river of song that caught up the best tunes from every

hand and linked them with the stubborn convictions and the most poignant longings of all the people.[7]

Albert (Panteleimon) Raboteau (1943–2021), Princeton professor emeritus and the author of *Slave Religion,*[*] was a convert to Orthodoxy through his studies. In his study of the slaves' practice of Christianity he notes one essential theme common to the Spirituals of the slaves and Orthodoxy: redemptive suffering. In the fourth century, St. Gregory the Theologian described the Faith as "suffering Orthodoxy." Every Sunday at Matins the Orthodox Church sings, "through the Cross joy has come into the world." In the classic Orthodox text on spiritual life, *The Ladder of Divine Ascent,* St. John Climacus entitles the seventh chapter "On Joy-making Mourning." He describes it as follows:

> Mourning according to God is sadness of soul and the disposition of a sorrowing heart, which ever madly seeks that for which it thirsts; and when it fails in its quest, it painfully pursues it, and follows in its wake grievously lamenting.[8]

On the slaves, Dr. Raboteau writes,

> Joyful sorrow, sorrowful joy, or more accurately sorrow merging into joy arose from the suffering of the slaves' lives, a suffering that was touched, however, and so transformed, by the living presence of God.[9]

This redemptive suffering, so central to the Negro Spirituals, is what has made their songs universal in scope and links them to Orthodoxy.

The white folk tradition of the Appalachians should also be recognized for its inherent musical and poetic value. The universal theme of suffering is prevalent in this tradition as well, in which it is called "sweet sorrow." The often parodied culture of the South has been heralded by highly-cultured

---

[*] Albert J. Raboteau, *Slave Religion: The "Invisible Institution" in the Antebellum South* (New York: Oxford University Press, 1978).

critics as the source of a unique and beautiful form of music, even though it is often caricatured and at the same time commercialized by the media. And while the black Spirituals and Appalachian Folk each constitute unique music genres in themselves, there also exists an interplay between the two. This social dynamic was exemplified in modern times in the Coen brothers' 2001 film *O Brother, Where Art Thou?* As par for Hollywood, the "hillbilly" is presented in this film as backward and laughable, while at the same time the soundtrack displays serious themes and musical virtuosity. The source of this culture is comprised of a black and white crossover in which clear demarcations are blurred.

Undoubtedly, there are many Orthodox who would balk at the notion of their sacred music being "tainted" by the strains of illiterate Negroes and hillbillies. But before making a judgment, it is suggested that one examine the method of the nationalist composers of Russia such as Glinka, Tchaikovsky, and Rimsky-Korsakov, who all incorporated the peasant folk music of their time into their great works. These composers incorporated folk elements into their music for precisely the same reason that folk elements were incorporated into Russia's liturgical music: This music reflected something elemental to the identity of the people.

Finally, Lomax discerned a direct relationship between the singing of the Appalachians and Slavic folk music when he wrote that the Sacred Harp* singers

> produce a sound that is like nothing else we have ever heard, unless it is the folk choirs of Southern Russia, at once strident and soaring, harmony without blend, polyphony† in the old Bachian sense.[10]

---

* "Sacred Harp" is a form of congregational hymn singing, originating in New England, but which found a home in the Southern states. It assigns specific, shaped note heads to different notes as an aid to sight reading. The "sacred harp" is the unaccompanied human voice.

† "Polyphony" is a complex harmony in which each part is a melodic line.

The Sacred Harp tradition is an early form of *a cappella** used in singing American hymns and Spirituals. It is performed in four-part harmony by groups of as many as 1,000 people at a time. There are regular "sing-ins" throughout the South and in some Northern states today.

The description which he gives concerning the way in which folk music develops over time is reminiscent of the process by which the Slavs adapted Byzantine music. This is especially poignant because he first contrasts this natural process with the artificial making of pop music. He writes that folk

> songs were accepted by whole communities, songs voted good by generations of singers and passed on by word of mouth to succeeding generations, a tradition quite different from popular song (made to sell and sell quickly) and cultivated art (made, so much of it, to conform to prestige patterns). If these songs had composers at first, they have largely been forgotten, and rightly so, since folk composers are adapters of old material rather than creators of original set pieces. The folk-ballad maker prefers to change an old song slightly to fit a new situation.[11]

This description also accords with another of Mark Bailey's precepts for composing (or adapting) new music: "Composers must strive to empty themselves of the compelling primary desire for self-expression."[12]

Hopefully, these considerations may lead one to at least a healthy respect for the American folk tradition, if not an appreciation of it. At the same time, we Americans may be surprised by the degree to which Church members from the Old Country perceive value in American culture. For example, in the late 19th century the great American novel by Harriet Beecher Stowe, *Uncle Tom's Cabin*, was printed in great quantities in Russia. In fact, this book played a significant role in the freeing of the serfs by Tsar Alexander II in 1861.[13]

---

* "*A cappella*" is singing "chapel-style," that is, without accompaniment by musical instruments.

Identity Crisis

SEVERAL AMERICAN ORTHODOX, in commenting on Fr. Freeman's article "Mission and Worship—America and the Orthodox," said that they valued the Sacred Harp tradition. One even conjectured that it would be the best of all genuine folk singing traditions that could be "baptizable" for use in Orthodox liturgical singing. However, he then observed that it would be too likely that it would not be a living tradition (because not many authentic Sacred Harp singers have converted to Orthodoxy). This is a common perception among American Orthodox who would desire a liturgical music common to their country. The attempt of converts in the Antiochian Archdiocese to adapt the liturgy directly to American classics like "Greensleeves" bears witness to this train of thought.

However, in the past, folk music was never simply "baptized" hook, line, and sinker. Rather, elements or phrases of national music were organically grafted into liturgical music. One should not lament the lack of living links with the American folk tradition. The tradition exists in the very fabric of our society and in ways which we cannot always recognize. These elements emerge when we look into our history, geography, and identity.

For example, the 1990 PBS documentary by Ken Burns on the Civil War naturally generated a soundtrack that, beyond the nostalgic associations of specific times and places, reflected our identity as Americans. And what the historian Shelby Foote says in this documentary in regard to the relationship between the Civil War and the American identity has far-reaching implications:

> Any understanding of this country has to be based on the Civil War. The Civil War defined us as what we are and it opened us up to what we became—both good and bad things. It is very necessary if you are going to understand the American character in the 20th century to learn of this enormous catastrophe of the 19th century. It was the crossroads of our being.[14]

While Orthodox Americans naturally adopt the historical legacy of Byzantium and Russia, they ought not to deny their own national legacy—either historical or cultural. To do so would be dishonest and false. Not a few American converts have experienced an acute identity crisis upon becoming Orthodox. Often, this occurs after failed attempts to become Grecophiles or Slavophiles. In the end, we all have to look in the mirror and come to grips with the world into which we were born. For this reason, it is imperative that Orthodox America be given the freedom to express its prayer with music that is inherently its own.

Towards American Orthodox Chant

ARCHIMANDRITE SERGIUS (BOWYER), Abbot of St. Tikhon's Monastery, and also music teacher at the Seminary, has often repeated in his lectures that throughout history the creative process in the liturgical arts often occurred in the monasteries. St. Romanos the Melodist, St. John of Damascus, St. Andrew of Crete, and St. Cassiana were all monastics. Liturgy is lived daily in the monasteries, and it is only natural that the development of chant would occur in an atmosphere where new music can be prayed out. Even in the monasteries deeply steeped in a specific liturgical form of chant—like those on Mount Athos, with its Byzantine musical tradition—there is an element of freedom both for variations within established modes and for composing new hymns.

Perhaps the greatest of all Athonite composers was the "Nightingale," St. John Koukouzelis. He was first a renowned singer in the Byzantine court. Later, as a monk on Mount Athos, he adapted the court style to serve the liturgical function.

More recently, a monk of Simonos Petras Monastery on Mount Athos put the devotional poem of St. Nectarios of Aegina, "O Pure Virgin," to music, making a "Byzantine Spiritual" that has become greatly popular in America and all over the world. The Oxford Byzantine scholar, Dimitri E.

Conomos, comments on why this particular hymn has been so widely received:

> "O Pure Virgin" can today be heard sung in Japanese, French, Tlingit, Italian, Russian, Swahili, Arabic, Romanian, English and many other languages. Its popularity is entirely due to the fact that it combines familiar elements of two musical cultures: the harmonic and metrical features of European lyrical ballads with the vocal production and exoticism that evokes a flavor of the East.[15]

BETWEEN 2003 AND 2007, a work of massive scope was conducted by Hieromonk Ephraim at St. Anthony's Monastery in Arizona. Fr. Ephraim devoted himself to translating into English and transcribing the Divine Services of the Byzantine Athonite tradition using Western notation. His monastic formation was on the Holy Mountain, hearing and singing these services before beginning this labor in America. He is a convert whose first language is English, which is important for translation which, ideally, is always into the mother tongue.

The quality of Fr. Ephraim's translation and wedding of text to music is truly amazing and instructive to contemporary liturgical composers. An example of the depth of Fr. Ephraim's work can be seen at the Divine Music Project website under the heading "Concerning Adaptation." He demonstrates how he works with ancient Byzantine music manuscripts, existing English translations each with its own strengths and weaknesses, and translations of the same hymn into several other languages. Through all this we can compare the different degrees to which the transcribers followed melodic patterns or adapted the melody to the text. Fr. Ephraim explains,

> In summary, the versions of this hymn written in countries where Byzantine chant has existed for centuries ... have two characteristics in common: the melody has been molded to match the text, and the text has not been tampered with in

order to fit a particular melody. On the other hand, most arrangements of this hymn from America—where Byzantine chant has only recently appeared—preserve characteristics of the original melody at the expense of the text.[16]

Finally, he tells us why he has chosen to make adaptations in the melody rather than the text: "we believe that the goal should be to alter or obscure the text as little as possible." In this, Fr. Ephraim is not just adhering to an ideal principle but is looking to the future with an inspired vision. That is, the purpose of Byzantine music is not to contribute to the creation and perpetuation of Old Country enclaves in America, but rather it is to be synthesized into English-speaking society.

While Fr. Ephraim has not published any new compositions, this does not necessarily mean that there can be no continuing process of adaptation with the Athonite Byzantine music. Conomos writes,

> What of the future? I believe that we shall observe a greater degree of choral singing as opposed to soloistic virtuosity—though the latter will not disappear entirely for some time. Athonite music will be greatly commercialized in the near future with the proliferation of CDs and chant anthologies beyond Greece. ... Western musical tendencies, though perhaps never acknowledged as such, may continue to blend with the chant. The Athonite musical tradition has adapted over the centuries to changing cultural tastes and conditions. This identifies it as an art that is living and flexible. At all events, because of its prestige, Athos will be a pace-setter for trends well beyond its own territory.[17]

So, in sum, while Fr. Ephraim has not written original compositions or worked with the American folk tradition, his work and shared wisdom are potentially a valuable foundation for those composers coming after him.

ONE AMERICAN MONASTIC who has composed liturgical hymns is Fr. Martin (Gardner). In 2007, St. John's Monastery in Manton, California, where Fr. Martin lived at the time, released a CD containing several of his original compositions. Fr. Martin is a third generation choir director but the first in his family to be Orthodox. In high school, he composed music for the piano. In college and graduate school, he studied linguistics rather than music. As an Orthodox he regularly attended the Summer Institute at St. Vladimir's Seminary. There, under the scrupulous ear of choir directors Dave Drillock and Mark Bailey, he first submitted an original communion hymn for Lazarus Saturday, and when this was received positively he continued to compose. He has also adapted a few standard Russian and Byzantine chants.

The link with American folk music is that Fr. Martin's pieces are composed on the pentatonic scale (1,2,3,5,6), as are many American folk songs—such as "Camp Town Races," "Shenandoah," and "Amazing Grace."* This scale is also common to Celtic folk music, reminding us that the roots of American music are deeply connected to the ballads and songs of the British Isles.

Fr. Martin's compositions were sung by the St. John's choir in a prayerful but unpretentious manner that could not be called "Protestant." However, perhaps due to the musical settings, there is something familiar about it to an American ear. Yet the "Anaphora," "It is Meet," and "Our Father" all stand out as pieces that could easily be adopted by choirs who draw primarily on the Russian tradition.

---

* "Amazing Grace" is a composed hymn that has been absorbed into Gospel, folk, and many other repertoires. The poem was penned in 1772, enshrining an inspired moment of repentance by Anglican clergyman John Newton. After his service in the Royal Navy he worked in the Atlantic slave trade. In 1748, in a severe and life-threatening storm at sea, he called out to God, beginning his steps toward conversion to Christ. As a Christian he also became an abolitionist. The melody we know today was composed in 1884 by William Walker.

Fr. Martin also interprets "Valaam Chant," popularized by Monk Herman of Valaam in the late 1990s. Here, his background in linguistics comes to "rescue" what is essentially "Russian Chant in English,"[18] making it authentic chant in the English language. The problem with "Russian Chant in English" is that when the Russian-speaking monks first translated the Slavonic hymns into English, the accents seemed to go everywhere except on the key words of the phrase! Our epidemic of "Russian Chant in English" has been a problem ever since Slavonic hymns began to be translated into English. It will be interesting now to see whether singers from other monasteries or parishes will place Fr. Martin's work into their own repertoires, or follow the pattern of putting new music to American settings, or both.

On the inlay of St. John's liturgical CD, Fr. Martin writes the following under the heading "Towards American Orthodox Chant":

> It is our monastery's vision that a uniquely American chant will gradually develop, growing up from the seeds of our inherited traditions. As they take root in American soil, this chant will become an organic hybrid of different influences from our own folk melodies and harmonies, rooted in the traditions of our ancestors, and drawing from the springs of the memorable melodies of the Carpatho-Rus' and the timeless and other-worldly modalities of Gregorian chant and its eastern counterpart, Byzantine chant.

ANOTHER MONASTIC COMPOSER is the African American nun, Mother Katherine (Weston) of the St. Xenia Monastic Community in Indianapolis. She has been active in the evangelical outreach to fellow African Americans through the Fellowship of St. Moses the Black and its annual conferences. Prior to composing liturgical music, Mother Katherine sang and recorded traditional Negro Spirituals and her own compositions as part of that outreach to youth and to people of color.

Just as black music has been at the center of creating unique forms of American music, so it would be expected that it would play a role in the development of American liturgical music. She will say more about this in her own chapter, following (p. 139).

Cross-cultural Synergy

WITHIN THE JURISDICTIONS of the Russian Church Abroad and the Antiochian Archdiocese there are a few parishes which use a form of Western Rite. One parishioner of St. Mark's in Denver describes their liturgical practice:

> We have Anglican chant from the St. Dunstan Psalter. We have hymns from the St. Ambrose hymnbook. We have hymns from the 1940 hymnal of the Episcopal Church, we have Gregorian Chant, and we have an excellent choir and a fabulous pipe organ. ... This form of Orthodoxy provides a great place for converts who treasure the great hymns of the faith from their past Protestant culture. ... It is difficult for some people to let go of the best things from their own heritage. Orthodoxy generously provides a way to retain the best things from our past Christian experience while learning the necessary corrections to false doctrine which our Orthodox Christian faith alone can provide.[19]

This man is obviously grateful to be in the Orthodox Church and not to have undergone a "Procrustean process" of conversion (i.e., forced cultural conversion). However, such a description does bring up questions as to how all these diverse liturgical elements are sewn together. Ideally, the Liturgy is a seamless whole, and it can be difficult to incorporate music of various traditions with continuity. Some former Anglicans who had interests in Western liturgical rites have opted, after giving the Western Rite a go, to adopt the practice of their local bishop. They preferred being a part of a living liturgical tradition, albeit of Eastern character, rather than having to recreate something that has been dormant for a long time.

It should also be remembered that as Elder Nectary of Optina said, "Orthodoxy is life," and therefore it is not only a set of correct dogmas. This "life" comes down in part through liturgical tradition. Nevertheless, in the case of St. Mark's in Denver, we may assume that the living Faith is being passed on, even as the parish members retain in their hearts certain aspects of Western Christian culture.

PERHAPS THE MOST widely embraced composition, based on cultural synergy, is the "American" or "Appalachian" setting for "Christ is Risen" (the Paschal troparion). This was composed by Dr. Vladimir Morosan, the Musical Director for St. Katherine Orthodox Mission in Carlsbad, California. He received his Doctorate in Choral Music and Musicology from the University of Illinois, and is a foremost authority on Russian choral music and Orthodox liturgical music. In his widely adopted "Christ is Risen," he brings together his own Russian background and expertise, with a pure American folk tradition. It is based on the pentatonic scale discussed above with reference to Fr. Martin's compositions, and is reminiscent of the Sacred Harp singing described above by Lomax.

IN ADDITION to fitting liturgical music to a specific purpose in worship, we should consider times during the Festal year into which new music naturally falls. The most obvious is, of course, Nativity. This is the time in which most Americans have grown up singing Christmas carols. However, caroling is by no means solely an American institution. Russians, Romanians, Greeks, Carpatho-Russians, etc., *all* sing carols.

A combined tradition has been followed for a fairly long period of time in some American monasteries. For example, in the early 1990s the nuns of Holy Nativity Convent in Boston made a beautiful recording which included Byzantine hymns for the Nativity and Christmas carols from America,

England, and Germany. At the St. Herman of Alaska Monastery in Platina, California, it has been the tradition for many decades to sing the 13th century Gregorian chant piece "O Come, O Come, Emmanuel" while venerating the icons after the conclusion of Compline* throughout the Nativity Fast. Throughout *Sviatiki,*† at the conclusion of Liturgy there is a procession with the star into the trapeza‡ accompanied by Christmas carols.

The practice of starring is most well-known, however, in the villages of Alaska. For the first three days of the Nativity Feast, each night after Vespers the star leads a procession to the homes of the faithful. There, each household prepares a table of food and the faithful sing carols and troparia, enjoy a brief visit, and then pass on to the next home. Over the course of the three days all the homes in the village are visited by the star.[20]

These various traditions, although "para-liturgical," can be of help in further expressing the joy of Christmas, in encouraging the faithful to bring the liturgical celebration into every aspect of life, and in promoting fellowship among the faithful. Otherwise, the fullness of the Orthodox way of life can be greatly threatened by the fast pace of modern American life. Finally, these are examples of inculturation in which the ethos of the liturgical celebration has not been altered.

Conclusions

IN LOOKING TO THE FUTURE of Orthodox liturgical music in America, perhaps it is best to consider first the role which music plays in our worship. Why is it so important? Dimitri Conomos offers the following:

---

* Compline is a liturgical service read after the evening meal and before bed.
† "Sviatiki" is the celebratory week after Nativity—up until the celebration of the Lord's circumcision on the eighth day.
‡ Trapeza is a monastic dining room, from the Greek word for "table."

It is precisely because it is an art of great subtlety and power which, when used incorrectly, can greatly distort or even caricature sacred poetry, but when understood properly, it can heighten the significance of the celebration, contribute to prayer, and emphasize the corporate nature of worship.

Music functions as a dramatic element—it has a unique and central place in the general structure of liturgy; it has acquired liturgical significance. Almost every word pronounced in church is 'sung' in one form or another. And the manner in which it is sung greatly affects the nature of the service. Week by week, season by season, the Church's song draws out the inner meaning of the liturgical poetry.[21]

In this respect, music overlaps with the essential task of the Church—to proclaim the Word of God, the Good News, to the faithful and to the entire world. And in this regard, we recall the work of the first apostolic community, from which members were sent to the ends of the earth. At the founding of this first community on the day of Pentecost, each one heard the Gospel in his own tongue (Acts 2:1–13). Therefore, this primary concern of communication should never be forgotten when we proclaim the Word. Like true theology, liturgical music must speak God's word to the people in a language and manner they can understand.

Thus, in our search for a liturgical music that resonates in the American soul, we can and should encourage the incorporation of the tonalities of American music. Of course, this is a delicate process and not one to be pursued by isolated individuals. For to be synthesized into the music of the Church, it must not only meet its functional criteria, but it must also be approved by those experienced members who have the discernment to recognize the essential qualities of genuine Orthodox liturgical expression.

Education in the field of America's cultural heritage can also aid the progress of liturgical music in an indirect way. If young people grow up with exposure to noble music and art, they will have a reference to the beauty in the Church. And if they learn to sing and dance, they will have gained a way to express the river of life which they feel within themselves. Finally, through an increase in cultural life within the parish, young and old will have a richer experience of the unity in community that lies at the heart of the Church. Such an existence may also be exactly what many Americans outside the Orthodox Church are looking for.

Like the spiritual renaissance that occurred in Orthodox lands in the 19th century, a renewal in liturgical and cultural life will only follow a renewal in spiritual life. The dynamic of this relationship is explained well by a holy man of recent times, St. Elder Paisios of Mount Athos:

> To chant right, our inner spiritual condition must be right. It is then that what reaches our ears is divine bliss. Christ fills the heart and the heart rejoices, and we turn and speak to God with a heart full of joy. And when we change from the heart, our heart is transformed; we feel the change and so do others around us.[22]

This clear and simple teaching of St. Paisios should remain as a final guideline to any music we sing in church, and especially in testing new music. While there are many other factors to consider, we should not lose sight of the fact that our song is an expression of prayer, which in turn is generated from the heart.

The Elder also reminds us, "To pray with the heart, we must hurt."[23] Our prayer and our music should not remain indifferent to the pain of the world (in which we, in our broken state, are included). For this reason, the Liturgy is replete with petitions for the sick and suffering, and for those who have passed on. This sensitivity to suffering mingled with heavenly joy can inspire the creativity of American Orthodox musicians. This ethos is consistent with the Orthodox music of the past. And as our liturgical music continues to develop, this ethos must always be present in order for our music to be authentic.

POSTSCRIPT

HIEROMONK ANDREW'S ARTICLE was originally published by St. Tikhon's Seminary in 2008, and information about musicians has been updated.[24] This postscript, supplied by Nun Katherine, brings the reader up to date on developments in American Orthodox Church music in the last 14 years, especially as it pertains to African American music forms.

A recent American convert to Orthodoxy, Dr. Shawn "Thunder" Wallace is Director of Jazz Studies at The Ohio State University; he is also Musical Director at Church of Christ of the Apostolic Faith in Columbus, Ohio. He has composed Orthodox liturgical music inspired by the Gospel music tradition that he grew up in. In February of 2020 he hosted an event called How Sweet the Sound, "showcasing a newly composed setting of an Orthodox Vespers in the style of black Gospel music." Dr. Wallace drew on melodies from black Gospel and Orthodox settings. His intent was to reveal the "unacknowledged connections" between the musical traditions and also to celebrate our "commonalities as Christians." The music was rendered by a Gospel choir, while talks on the significance of the endeavor were given by two speakers: Fr. Moses Berry, now President Emeritus of the Fellowship of St. Moses the Black, and Dr. Peter C. Bouteneff, Professor of Systematic Theology at St. Vladimir's Orthodox Seminary.[25] It will be interesting to see further developments, either from Wallace himself, or other musicians inspired by him.

BENEDICT SHEEHAN is, perhaps, the most widely-known Orthodox composer in America to use folk elements or "Americana." Among other things, Sheehan is Director of Music and Assistant Professor of Liturgical Music at St. Tikhon's Seminary. He is also the founder and conductor of two professional choirs that perform in both concert and liturgical settings: the St. Tikhon Choir and Artefact Ensemble. He graciously agreed to be represented in this volume, providing written material and making time for an informal interview to give the following portrait of his current work.

Reflecting on the question of what the music of Orthodox Christians in America should be, Sheehan asks, "Should it be based on folk music and Spirituals?"* Then he asks whether it should be inspired by the traditions of Protestant hymn singing, black Gospel music, or something else. So we see that in his thinking, as in Hieromonk Andrew's, these components of the African American musical tradition are appropriate sources of inspiration for American Orthodox music. In response to my question as to whether he in fact used American folk elements in his own compositions, he said,

> Yes, I definitely incorporate elements of Americana, generally speaking, into my liturgical works. I do this consciously in some instances, but unconsciously in many others. I actually think the unconscious influence is sometimes stronger, and more musically satisfying, but I do it quite deliberately as well.[26]

Some years ago, he took to heart the lament of a black seminarian at St. Tikhon's who said that missionary outreach to black Americans was hampered by the fact that the usual Orthodox church music, as beautiful as it may be, doesn't "feel like church" to his people. Sheehan sympathized with the problem, but had no ready solution to offer. Therefore, when Dr. Shawn Wallace debuted his Orthodox Vespers in the Gospel idiom, described above, Sheehan, although not able to attend, still listened to the recordings with interest. He was very pleased conceptually with the work and, later on, was also pleased to learn of my own liturgical compositions based on Negro Spiritual melodies.

---

* From the foreword to Sheehan's Liturgy No. 2. This was commissioned by St. Michael Church in Lexington, Kentucky, in honor of its former pastor, Fr. Alexander Atty (1951–2014). He brought together a harmonious and diverse parish, and ensured that the various ethnicities were represented in worship. Later he became Dean of St. Tikhon's, where Sheehan knew him personally.

Conversing about music naturally led to the topic of liturgical texts. There have been times of the flowering of Orthodox hymnography, such as the sixth through the eighth centuries in Byzantium, and another period before the fall of Constantinople. Later in the 18th century, Russian hymnographers were inspired by the form of the akathist hymn and produced a great many akathists in praise of saints, angels, liturgical feasts, icons, as well as to the Lord and His Mother. He hopes that there will be a new flowering of Orthodox hymnography as well as music composition. For, while many parts of the Divine Liturgy are fixed, some areas, such as the antiphons and the communion hymns, invite ongoing creativity. And this remains true of hymns used for other services or private prayer such, again, as the akathist. He found our own *Akathist to the Merciful Savior: Healer of the Wounds of American Slavery* [27] to be inspiring.

Another important aspect of liturgical texts for composers and adapters is the question of when to adapt the text to the cadence of the music, and when to adapt the music to the existing text. Sheehan is aware of the need at times to consult multiple translations, and would potentially welcome some fresh translations. Robert Alter, for example, created a literary translation of the entire Hebrew Bible, [28] with an eye to bringing the poetic feel of the original Hebrew into English. There is so much more to liturgical translation than mere accuracy of words; the poetry of the original functions much like music itself to stir the soul to prayer.

SHEEHAN IS NOT ONLY synthesizing elements of American culture into his liturgical music, he is also bringing Orthodox ethos into the world through public performances of his liturgical settings as, for example, his Liturgy of St. John Chrysostom, No. 1.* He describes this Liturgy as

---

* The Liturgy No. 1 was commissioned by the Patriarch Tikhon Russian-American Music Institute™ (PaTRAM Institute™).

the Orthodox musical tradition filtered through my own experience, background, and musical sensibilities. It is at once both deeply personal and broadly expansive, a sort of musical universe that kept expanding outwards to include more and more of what—and who—I know and love.[29]

In a non-liturgical performance of this Liturgy on February 18, 2022, Austin-based professional choir Conspirare,* premiered Sheehan's setting of "Credo,"† a prose poem by W. E. Burghardt Du Bois.[30]‡ In this particular concert, "Credo" occupied the place of the Nicene Creed which, incidentally, had not been set to music in Sheehan's original score. To Sheehan, the significance of using "Credo" in the context of the Liturgy was that he had

> long felt a desire to grapple with issues of racial injustice and inequality through the medium of, or at least in the context of, Orthodox liturgical music, and setting Du Bois's text seemed to me the perfect way to do that.[31]

He further sees Du Bois's "Credo" as an eloquent statement of the value of the human person, which Orthodox Christians understand through the lens of the icon: that each person is an icon of our Lord Jesus Christ. Sheehan adds,

> I offer "Credo" as a symbol of faith—and of hope and love as well—set in the midst of my liturgy. My goal here is not to replace the church's own statement of faith, but to assert that, for my own part, I also believe in the human person, and especially those who are downtrodden, suffering, and oppressed.[32]

---

* Craig Hella Johnson is the founder and conductor of Conspirare, which began in 1991. It is based in Austin, Texas.

† "Credo" was commissioned by Conspirare as a counterpoint to their performance, during the same week, of Margaret Bonds's setting of "Credo." Margaret Bonds (1913–1972) was a prominant African American composer.

‡ "Credo" appears in Du Bois's work, *Darkwater: Voices from Within the Veil.*

In reflecting on this Liturgy in its concert presentation, I am reminded of how pivotal it was, in my own journey towards Orthodoxy, to sing in an amateur choir that performed Rachmaninoff's "All Night Vigil" in various non-liturgical settings, including outdoors in a redwood forest. We don't know what seeds are planted in people's hearts, whether they be singers or listeners. We do know that Christ is Beauty, and that encounters with the beauty of the Church, through music, architecture, or icons, can be transformative.

Sheehan is also planning a collaborative venture with an African American Gospel musician to create a public memorial service marrying elements of the Gospel musical tradition with elements of the Orthodox liturgical tradition, to create something new and memorable. Sheehan says he hopes to present this service in a public performance in March of 2024, in conjunction with the four-year anniversary of Breonna Taylor's death. I really look forward to hearing that.

LAST BUT IN NOWISE LEAST is nazo zakkak, a Lebanese American composer who began with a bachelor's in Jazz Studies from San Diego State and then earned an MFA in Integrated Composition, Improvisation, and Technology from UC Irvine. Though he is cradle Orthodox, it was while working as a music proofreader that he fell in love with Orthodox liturgical music, internalizing it more deeply in this manner. He has studied Byzantine chant, Russian chant, Gregorian chant, and Renaissance counterpoint. But his goal is to further develop an American Orthodox musical identity. His first piece, a Great Doxology, premiered at St. Vladimir's Orthodox Theological Seminary in 2012. Since then, parishes and monasteries have been commissioning his hymns. Composer Kurt Sander says that

> zakkak's work is neither traditional nor contemporary; and yet, neither is it somewhere in between. Instead, it

lies somewhere completely outside of these two polarities, and for an Orthodox composer, perhaps this is the best place to be.*

When I described to zakkak our vision for this book, and especially this chapter, he responded,

> This sounds like an amazing and fruitful project. I am happy to contribute in any way that I can. The topic of American Orthodox music has been of great fascination to me; yet I don't get the chance to speak freely about it. For the past few years I've actually been using the 1867 *Slave Songs of the United States* anthology as source material for some hymns. It is a subject for which I care deeply and think about daily.

zakkak graciously gave me an informal interview. His childhood was shaped by serving in the altar and by piano lessons. But also during those years, he learned about the Underground Railroad and developed a fascination for the stories and the history of that period of American life. He became acquainted with the music of the Underground Railroad and this became a door to the appreciation of Spirituals and African American music and culture in general.

He has become a student of world music, and is familiar with the patterns of African music as well. (Speaking of world music, he has also been commissioned by the Chinese Language Division of Ancient Faith to compose the first ever Divine Liturgy for Mandarin speakers.)

Let's go deeper into how he uses the Negro Spirituals as an inspiration for Orthodox liturgical composition. Many people, he states, have noted that his music sounds "American Orthodox." He searched to find an authentic resource for this, just as the Octoechos† has been for any Orthodox

---

* http://www.nazozakkak.com/about-1

† The "Octoechos" or book of the eight tones, has the basic melodies used for Orthodox worship in an eight-week, rotating cycle. There are many special melodies and arrangements of music used as well.

composer. It was at this point, in 2018, that he discovered *Slave Songs of the United States,* which contains melodies for 136 hymns. He began memorizing them immediately— "this is what my jazz training taught me." And then he spent a year singing them to himself, internalizing them deeply, before beginning his first composition. Occasionally he will base a liturgical piece on a single melody, but most often, fragments of melody, like musical words, will come forward "because it was my language."

He notes that using the melodies is challenging. "The music is rhythmic, incredibly rhythmic, and repetitive. Bulgarian music also has those elements, but expressed in a different way." He notes that in Byzantine liturgical music, notably in the canons, there is a deep poetic structure to the verses. There is meter and often an acrostic tying all the verses together into a single prayer. For that reason, he shares the frustration of other composers and adapters with the current state of English-language translations. They often focus on "accuracy" to the detriment of poetry. And yet there is meaning embedded in poetic form which is lost by that approach. zakkak's "secret" or "passion" project is the composition of an entire Divine Liturgy, based on the Spirituals. He played one piece from it for me and it brought tears in my eyes.

I raised the question of a common feature of the Spirituals and how this makes standard Western harmonization difficult. This is the feature of going down, up, and down a third interval. (For example, the first four notes of "Swing Low, Sweet Chariot.") He replied that this is a common feature of African music that has been retained in the Spirituals. Sometimes his answer to the difficulties of harmonization is simply to provide a unison melody. He is mindful of the choir of one or two voices—what can they do beautifully? If they want to improvise harmony, that also fits the ethos of the Spirituals and the ethos of Orthodox liturgical singing.

zakkak has also experimented with a different conducting style during Liturgy. Instead of using a musical arrangement with all the vocal entrances and exits scripted out, he selected a very simple score. Then using gestures from jazz conducting, he improvised a one-time arrangement, just for that liturgical moment.

zakkak has been hurt to see the African American family that comes once to services, never to return, and is concerned that music may be part of the reason. He wants to help, and also not to misappropriate the Spirituals. I encouraged him, by all means, to continue what he is doing and, perhaps, to compose some hymns that were more explicit in their musical reference to the Spirituals. This is welcome and much needed.

Choirs

I WOULD BE REMISS in closing without mentioning the choirs that are bringing contemporary American Orthodox music to life. First and foremost, ordinary Orthodox church choirs and their conductors have adopted scores from Sheehan and zakkak, or pieces such as Dr. Vladimir Morosan's American "Christ is Risen," or Fr. Martin's scores—"It is Truly Meet" and others. (Fr. Martin's scores have the hallmark designation "Tonus Americanus" where one would expect the composer's name.) The St. Athanasius Orthodox Church Choir recorded a CD in 2017* including several by nazo zakkak and other contemporary composers. I should also point out the various church choirs singing hymns that were unassumingly composed or adapted by their own clergy or choir conductors. An example is the Trisagion which was adapted from the shape note melody "Star in the East" by Mark King.

The Illinois Orthodox Choir, an amateur community choir founded and conducted by Dr. Zhanna Lehmann, has premiered and recorded some of my compositions. The Spirit of Orthodoxy Choir, directed by Stratos J. Mandalakis, is based in the New York-New Jersey area. This choir is now adding some

---

* *Sing to the Lord a New Song*, Valerie Yova, conducting.

of my pieces to its repertory. nazo zakkak released a CD of his compositions, *Luxari*, in 2016. (The album is sung by the Adelphos Ensemble, a secular choir.) Benedict Sheehan has founded two professional choirs: the St. Tikhon Choir and Artefact Ensemble. The former has sung his Liturgy in the celebration of the Eucharist. The latter, comprised of artists from all across the country, has performed his work primarily on the concert stage. And he is not limited to conducting his own choirs, but also guest conducts, introducing a wider group of singers and listeners to contemporary Orthodox music. Thanks to these and other choral groups, American Orthodox music, in all its variety, is helping the faithful to lift up their hearts during the divine services and is also available for listening at other times through concerts and recordings. The right music for the moment helps us to attune our spirits to the divine, and aids our striving to pray always.

8

A BRIEF HISTORY OF SPIRITUALS AND GOSPEL MUSIC

NUN KATHERINE WESTON

T HE FELLOWSHIP HAS BEEN SINGING African American Spirituals and learning about their significance since the '90s. Let's look at them now in their historical context—what characterizes the Spirituals and how were they preserved? And how are they related to Gospel music?

Starting with the first question, West Africans sang in their homelands, and in captivity they brought their music with them to the Americas. Here, they continued to sing a variety of songs—work songs, lamentations ... songs in their original languages, songs in their adopted languages. During the first centuries of slavery, preaching the Gospel to enslaved Africans was sometimes explicitly forbidden, or it was practiced in a limited way, focusing on the slaves' duty of obedience. However, during the Great Awakening of the 18th and 19th centuries, the Gospel of Jesus Christ was preached on a new, more egalitarian basis, with a new focus on personal experience as the source of spiritual authority. People attended revivals regardless of caste or class—white, black, indigenous—all people were welcome. The enslaved blacks took elements from their own music and from the Protestant hymns they were exposed to, creating something new and unique. This was the first truly original music form for the US, the Negro Spiritual.

Although the revivals were racially mixed, the churches that people returned to were not likely to be. Even if they had sections for whites and for blacks, the enslaved still sought the freedom to worship and sing from the heart without observation or censure. Thus, Africans in the Americas enjoyed all their types of song in the enclosure of their own living and work spaces. Because of segregation, their music was not widely known outside of those cultural spaces—in the 1860s, that changed suddenly and dramatically.

It's easy to imagine that there was simply an unbroken oral/aural* tradition of singing Spirituals in the South that followed the diaspora of free black people during the Great Migration.† But the history of these songs is more interesting than that. In freedom, some African Americans saw the old songs as something to shed—as part of the stigma of a history of enslavement. And even when the songs were handed down, how did they avoid evolution? How did they come to be transcribed and put in anthologies, just as they were sung in the years after emancipation?

Three things contributed substantially to the writing down and the dissemination of the old slave songs, especially those that came to be known as Spirituals or "jubilee songs." These were, first, the collecting of songs on the Sea Islands off the coasts of South Carolina and Georgia; second, African American college choirs; and third, the proliferation of black singing troupes.

Since the American Missionary Association (AMA) was involved in the education of freedmen and thus with the

---

* "Aural" means "by hearing."
† The Great Migration began with the institution of Jim Crow laws in the South, and continued from 1916–1970.

collecting and performance of Spirituals, let's pause and get acquainted with it. The AMA was founded in 1846 by Protestant abolitionists, merging three recent missionary organizations that all had an anti-slavery stance. They founded it because the well-established missionary organizations were indifferent, at best, to the question of slavery. From the beginning of the Civil War, the AMA began to open schools for the new freedmen. By the close of the 1860s they had chartered seven schools of higher education, based on successful models used at that time in the North. They taught academic and trade curricula, and especially focused on educating a new generation of black teachers. The first schools were in Virginia, Kentucky, Tennessee, Louisiana, Mississippi, Alabama, and Georgia.

The fruitful collaboration between Spiritual-singing freedmen and white musicians began on St. Helena, one of the Sea Islands off the coast of South Carolina. There, through the efforts of government functionaries, the AMA, and other private philanthropies, schools were set up for freedmen right after the Battle of Port Royal in 1861. Three musically trained Northerners came to the island for different humanitarian reasons: William Francis Allen, a scholar and teacher; Charles Pickard Ware, a superintendent of freedmen plantations; and Lucy McKim Garrison, who was there as her father's secretary. They all joined forces in their interest in collecting and preserving the songs they heard from the new freedmen. Their work eventually led to the publication of *Slave Songs of the United States* in 1867.[1] Part of their motivation, as abolitionists, was to demonstrate to Northern citizens the indelible humanity of black people as shown through their spirituality, their music, and their creativity. The anthology contains 136 songs.

The Spirituals, in their natural element, were sung in a participatory way, without audience. Thus, the purpose of their singing style was to maximize the experience of the participants. It was neither in unison, nor in Western harmonies, familiar to us through Protestant hymns or Russian-style

Orthodox choral singing. Singers each found their melodic stream as they felt led by the Spirit, accompanied by the clapping of hands. The typical clapping rhythm on the Sea Islands was | <u>1</u> 2 3 <u>4</u> | <u>1</u> 2 <u>3</u> 4 | (also familiar to us as the Calypso beat of the West Indies). This is the culture the St. Helena musician-missionaries encountered; understandably, they transcribed only a single melodic line, preserving some of the flavor of the Gullah dialect as they captured the lyrics.

The second factor that led to the dissemination of jubilee songs and their singing was the establishment of colleges for freedmen, most notably Fisk in Nashville, Tennessee (1865) and the Hampton Institute in Hampton, Virginia (1868). These were both launched by the American Missionary Association, but the schools had to develop their own funding. Fisk soon found itself in dire financial straits. The treasurer, George L. White, who also doubled as singing instructor, formed a choir to raise funds through their concerts.* Although they began with a repertoire of Western music, he realized they could really distinguish themselves by bringing the Spirituals to the stage.

White (of European heritage) gathered Spiritual songs from the students and set them to four-part harmonies. He wanted them to appear as dignified and impressive as possible to Northern white audiences, so the customary hand clapping and stepping to the music were avoided. Although they initially went through months of hardship and setbacks, the Fisk Jubilee Singers finally reached a turning point. This required further assistance from the AMA, which helped them secure engagements and good press in New York and Boston. After this they packed opera houses, raised more than enough for Fisk's basic expenses—$150,000 in their seven years—and procured handsome gifts from manufacturers to furnish many of the campus's needs. What they offered to

---

* The initial choir members were: Ella Sheppard, Maggie L. Porter, Jennie Jackson, Minnie Tate, Eliza Walker, Phoebe J. Anderson, Thomas Rutling, Benjamin M. Holmes, Greene Evans, Isaac P. Dickerson, and George Wells.

the Christian society who embraced them was clean and wholesome entertainment. (We may well ask what was lost and what was gained by using hymns in this way.) In 1892 *The Story of the Jubilee Singers*[2] was first published. This volume contained a history of their first six years on tour and an anthology of 139 of their songs with choral arrangements. It also broadened the reach of the Spirituals.

Hampton followed suit in forming a choir in 1873. Their choir director, Thomas Fenner (also of European ancestry) wanted to differentiate them from their rival. He was also more sensitive than his counterpart at Fisk to the black students' musical heritage, and so he sought a more authentic sound in his musical arrangements. Instead of the Western four-part harmony, he sometimes scored out as many as seven vocal lines. He kept more dialect and more of the vocal slides and other hallmarks of the original field singing.[3] The original Hampton Singers were a troupe of 17. In the early years they managed to raise some $300,000 for the school. Hampton Institute eventually published "Fifty Cabin and Plantation Songs" in a book called *Hampton and Its Students*.[4] As more and more historically black colleges and universities were founded, they also had choirs, but did not necessarily go on tour.

Finally, the third factor in disseminating the Spirituals was that many jubilee choirs sprang up, inspired perhaps, by Fisk and Hampton, but not affiliated. These included the Tennesseans, the Original Nashville Students, the Williams Jubilee Singers from Chicago, and the Albert McNeil Jubilee Singers from Los Angeles. The North Carolinians and the Wilmington Jubilee Singers from the same state, not only sang, but offered demonstrations of slave life on stage—this was part of the movement for "authenticity" in the Spirituals' performance.[5]

Gospel Music

HOW, THEN, did Gospel music originate? The music of slavery days was folk music—anonymously composed and reworked. After emancipation, Spirituals were adapted to the new life in freedom. During the Great Migration, six million black Americans migrated north and west. They also migrated from the context of small rural churches in the South to small storefront churches in dense, urban areas. As an urban culture for black people developed, so the singing of Spirituals began the metamorphosis into the Gospel style.[6] This entailed a shift from strictly congregational singing to forming choirs and quartettes.* And along with these groups came tighter harmonies and sometimes, the addition of instruments. During these transitional years there were also black composers who published four-part hymns with the feel of Spirituals. Now archived scores allow us to still see how these composers envisioned their own harmonies. Sam Lucas (c. 1848–1916), who started publishing in the 1870s, was one such popular composer.

Just as the Spirituals were sung in church and also performed on stage, so it was with Gospel music. Most Gospel songs were composed, and the singer songwriters could become famous recording artists. After the Gospel style matured, sometimes the only difference between a Spiritual and a Gospel song was the rendition—Gospel groups like the Fairfield Four recorded a number of Spirituals. Gospel music, which had been gradually evolving, became popular in the 1930s, during the Great Depression. This bleak time hit all Americans hard, especially those who did not have much to begin with. The new music was a sustaining force in lives of many black Americans.

During the '30s, three musical streams converged to create what we recognize as Gospel: first, there was the exuberant worship style of the Holiness-Pentecostal churches; second, there was the solo-style of Gospel singing that emerged in the South, in tandem with blues singing; and third, there was the musical contribution of Charles Tindley (1851–1933).[7]

The Rev. Tindley was a remarkable man—unable to attend seminary, he educated himself through correspondence

---

* Not always strictly four singers.

courses and other means, excelling on the commissioning exam for the Methodist ministry. Tindley was also a musician; like Sam Lucas, above, Tindley composed choral hymns based on the Spirituals. He wrote hymns that addressed the day-to-day struggles of ordinary Christians. He added instruments, improvisation, and blue notes (flattened thirds, sevenths, or fifths), giving his hymns a unique sound.[8] He composed dozens of Gospel songs.

Thomas Dorsey (1899–1993)* is called the father of Gospel music. He was a pastor's son who made a name for himself in jazz and blues. He also tried composing church music using those secular idioms, often meeting resistance from pious people. He went through dark depressions followed by a spiritual awakening. "It was Tindley's music that brought Thomas Dorsey back into the church from the Vaudeville circuit, nightclubs and taverns,"[9] according to one of Tindley's pastoral successors. Dorsey built on Tindley's style, "baptizing" jazz and blues elements. When he wrote "Take My Hand, Precious Lord," the new Gospel style took flight, gaining widespread popularity. He went on to compose perhaps hundreds of Gospel hymns.

In addition to Thomas Dorsey, Mahalia Jackson (1911–1972) and Sister Rosetta Tharpe (1915–1973)—known for her electric guitar playing—helped popularize Gospel music. Dorothy Love Coates (1928–2002) with the Gospel Harmonettes is not as well known today, but she was a prolific songwriter who influenced and inspired other artists—but for all that, she remained poor and humble. Dn. John Gresham says more about her in his chapter (p. 85).

Blues, jazz, and Spirituals all have their root in the music of the enslaved, and Gospel assimilates all those elements to form something at once both new and ancestral. It uses call and response from West African heritage, handed down through the Spirituals. It also conserves the blue notes from jazz.

---

* Not to be confused with jazz trombonist Tommy Dorsey (1905–1956).

This is the image I would like to leave you with: The whole history of Spirituals and Gospel music looks like an elaborate family tree, with branchings and intermarriages. The slave songs form the trunk of the tree, with roots in West African rhythms and call-and-response patterns mentioned above. Other roots are in the Gospel of Jesus Christ and, finally, in Protestant hymn-singing. From the slave-song trunk, we have the branches of Spirituals, work songs, and blues. The Spiritual genre intermarried with Western musical notation, four-part harmonies, and the formation of singing troupes to produce a performance style of Spiritual music. The tradition of solo blues singing with guitar and harmonica, intermarried with the brass band, and various other music styles, to yield jazz. The Spiritual, blues, and jazz genres recombined, yielding Gospel. Performers who began with Gospel diversified into soul and pop; performers who began in jazz moved into hymn singing. All of this has worked together to create a rich musical heritage. And now, American Orthodox composers are looking to that heritage for inspiration, and to bring the firstfruits of the musical harvest to Christ.

9

SPIRITUALS

A WELLSPRING
FOR ORTHODOX
LITURGICAL MUSIC

NUN KATHERINE WESTON

Their sound hath gone forth into all the earth
And their words unto the ends of the world

—Psalm 19:4

T HE MEMORY LEAPS OUT TIMELESSLY, although it was June 24, 2005. Denver was hosting the St. Moses the Black Conference with guest speaker, Fr. Martin Ritsi; his presentation was on "The Church in Africa: Missions, Development, and Growth." During the Q&A, he surprised us with an unexpected and prescient invitation—could we use our rich heritage of Spirituals as a basis for new compositions of Orthodox liturgical music? This would be missions work of a different kind from his, but just as important in our own field. The invitation sparked excited conversations and impromptu renditions of possibilities. Fr. Martin was not the first, by any means, to point out the kinship between the traditions—

there is a commonality of sorrowful joy, a shared heritage of suffering Christianity between the Orthodox and the enslaved Christians in the Americas.[1]

The challenge readily imbued us with a sense of mission and hope—the hope that African Americans in the Orthodox Church could "baptize" an aspect of our religious tradition, offering it back to Christ in a new form. We hoped for the evangelical message to be translated into the music of our people as an invitation for others of African descent to discover the beauties of the Orthodox Faith.

But even given these noble aspirations, was our project respectful of Orthodox tradition? And is there any precedent for the incorporation or synthesis of folk melodies into Orthodox liturgical music? Yes: Some of the melodies used for everyday Orthodox liturgical chant* have a folk-melody component. For example, with the baptism of Serbia, Orthodox chant was adopted there and passed down orally. In this way, it was gradually inculturated to the traditional Serbian folk music—this process is also referred to as the "baptism of culture." Later in the late 19th century, Stevan Stojanović Mokranjac, the "father of Serbian music," wrote down the received melodies in Western musical notation. Byzantine chant in Russia underwent a similar transformation. In addition, 19th century Russian composers such as Mikhail Glinka, Pyotr Tchaikovsky, and Nikolai Rimsky-Korsakov sometimes incorporated bits of folk melody in their liturgical compositions, just as a poet might make a literary allusion to a myth or to another poem.

From Proof-of-Concept to Concert

AFTER DENVER, I arrived home inspired—I began to further develop a musical idea from the trip. What I bring to the endeavor are a love of the Spirituals, and also decades of

---

* This refers to the music of the eight tones used in Orthodox liturgical worship.

leading Orthodox liturgical music from the kliros.* I bring a lifetime of immersion in choir—and sometimes solo—singing, and a lifetime hobby of musical notation. Compared with the talented and academically trained composers in our Faith, I am something of an outsider artist. But that endows me the freedom to approach the Spirituals first and foremost on their own terms, through their own history. Only then do I seek to marry that legacy with Western choral traditions.

My initial work was really proof-of-concept, as I was not a choir conductor working towards actual performances. My earliest piece, an Anaphora, was sung at Fellowship conferences. This was not in the context of liturgy, but as part of our musical programming. It was only incrementally that I began to dialogue with choir directors and musicians. They had a number of very helpful suggestions for the harmonies as well as equipping me with language to discuss what I had been doing implicitly and intuitively. We began discourse about reasonable vocal ranges for amateur choirs, and we experimented with key transpositions. In short, the work was moving from proof-of-concept to the possibility of live choral performance. This, in fact, took place on December 5, 2021, when Dr. Zhanna Lehmann, founder and conductor of the Illinois Orthodox Choir, included three of my pieces in her Christmas concert. She also kindly arranged for this to be recorded so that people could listen for themselves and discern if they wanted to use these pieces.†

I have a few compositions to date. The first, in 2005 as mentioned above, was an Anaphora based on the Spiritual melody "Were You There When They Crucified My Lord?" The second, in 2019, was a Cherubic Hymn based on the melody "Sometimes I Feel Like a Motherless Child." Then in

---

* The kliros is a stand, usually toward the front of an Orthodox church, where readers and cantors lead the singing and the responses to the clergy.

† The recordings and scores are available at http://mosestheblack.org/resources/our-music.

2021, the "Our Father" was based on the melody "Balm in Gilead." Now in 2022, I've worked on a Polyeleos inspired by "Couldn't Hear Nobody Pray" and a Trisagion based on "You Hear the Lambs a-Cryin."

A Roadmap

HERE IS WHERE my process began: I contemplated Spirituals which I already knew and loved, and combed through recordings of the Fisk Jubilee Singers and other choirs and quartets. I looked for Spirituals of a slow and measured tempo. This eliminated a large selection, which are fast-tempoed, hand-clapping melodies. On the other hand, it can be interesting, musically, to shift the tempo when making musical arrangements. While I didn't always use a melody in its entirety, the whole composition was based on one melody. There could be other ways to compose—for example, a medley approach or composing original melodies based on the Spiritual esthetic.

I searched for melodies based on stepwise melodic progressions;* this is both a foundation of Western music theory, and what we are most accustomed to in Orthodox music. We encounter stepwise progressions in the Byzantine family of melodies and in the Russian four-part choral works. But many of the Spiritual melodies (in common with Sacred Harp† melodies), are based on expanded chords‡ or arpeggios. This gives the melodies a very different feel, requiring a different approach to harmony. And because such melodies often require a wide vocal range, adaptations have to be made for choral singing. I will say more about that below.

---

* An example of a stepwise tonal progression is C-D-E-F-G. Using the abbreviation "m" for "minor," its chord progression might be C G C Fm C.

† The "Sacred Harp" is the human voice. This *a cappella* music is pentatonic.

‡ An example of an expanded tonal progression or arpeggio is C-E-G-E-G. Its chord progression might be C C G C G. Or it could just stay on the C chord. Stepwise progressions offer opportunity for more varied and intricate chord progressions than expanded ones.

I also looked for songs whose familiar lyrics would make sense in terms of how their music was repurposed. For example, the hymn's first line, "Were you there when they crucified my Lord?" is actually answered by the anaphora for which I set it: "For as often as you eat this bread and drink from this cup, you proclaim the Lord's death until he comes" (1 Cor 11:26). So "yes," we are saying to our ancestors, "I was there—I am there—when they crucified our Lord, as often as I participate in the Holy Liturgy. And I am bringing you with me in my heart."

Likewise, the lament, "Sometimes I feel like a motherless child, a long, long way from home," is answered in its setting of the Cherubic Hymn. For that hymn enjoins us to lay down every earthly care, even the heavy cares of orphanhood. We are orphans no more because the Church is our loving mother. We are orphans no more, for we greet our Creator, the Lover of mankind as He arrives, borne up by the angelic hosts.

The third is the "Our Father," set to the tune of "Balm in Gilead." The original Spiritual makes answer to Jeremiah 8:22, "Is there no balm in Gilead? Is there no physician there?" The Spiritual proclaims that, yes, "there is a balm in Gilead to make the wounded whole." The balm is our Lord Jesus Christ, and it is His saving ministry. In using the melody as a basis for the "Our Father," we are saying, furthermore, that there is no balm like the prayer which flowed from His lips when His disciples asked Him, "Lord, teach us to pray" (Lk 11:1).

"You Hear the Lambs a-Cryin'" works beautifully with the Trisagion. The song is a tender dialogue between the Lord and Peter, based on John 21:17. First, "You hear the lambs a-cryin' [3x], O Shepherd, feed-a My sheep," is sung, as from the mouth of Christ; then Peter assures Him of his loyalty. Until the flock encounters Christ, its voice is a wordless cry. Now we, as liturgical Christians, are rational sheep. Our cries are no longer wordless, but we cry, "Holy God, Holy Mighty,

Holy Immortal, have mercy on us!" And to this rational cry of the flock, the Lord tells Peter, "Feed My sheep on the sweet grass of true doctrine and on My body and blood." Since Orthodox music should clothe and enhance the words of prayer, I have put much thought into the congruence of the original lyrics of the Spiritual hymn and the Orthodox prayer that will find a new home in its melody.

NOW, LET'S LOOK at how another composer used a Western melody as a basis for Orthodox music: One of the best-loved non-liturgical Orthodox hymns, "O Pure Virgin," was based on the melody "Greensleeves." The poem was written by St. Nektarios of Aegina, but was set to music by Hieromonk Gregory of Simonopetra Monastery. He overheard pilgrims singing "Greensleeves" while in the Holy Land and thought the melody would be perfect to adapt to St. Nektarios's poem.

More for Musicians

In adapting the melody to a Byzantine aesthetic, Fr. Gregory had to keep this in consideration: Orthodox music uses modal scales* called "tones." But unlike Western music, which is based on the major and minor keys—two modes—there are eight Byzantine tones, and none of these corresponds to our major key. Western harmonies are based on chords that progress and resolve. Not so with Byzantine music. Sometimes harmonies consist of parallel thirds and sometimes they are predominantly drone notes or "isons." Fr. Gregory, therefore, was free in his adaptation. We recognized the rhythm of "Greensleeves" right away. The first and second melodic movements seem to be based on the melody of the verse; the third melodic movement might be based on the chorus.

For his adaptation, Fr. Gregory took the nine-note range of the original melodic progression and compressed it into a

---

* The tones or modes are scales, each with a distinctive pattern of intervals between each note.

144

five-note range, to make it more flowing and Byzantine feeling. Greensleeves, below:

became this as a Byzantine melody,* developing on what could be an alto harmony line of the original:

So, if we distill a few principles from Fr. Gregory, they might be summed up thus: First, a Western melody may be used for inspiration, rather than using it note for note. Second, it is actually possible to transform a Western melody into one of the Byzantine tones, using isons to accompany it. Third, in making that transformation, the melody may be compressed to make it more flowing. This gives us more tools to work with and may reveal more Spiritual melodies as candidates for repurposing than I originally thought. On the other hand, such melodies might be rendered unrecognizable, but our goal is to retain the flavor of the original Spirituals.

UNLIKE FR. GREGORY, my monastic formation was based on the eight-tone system of Russian liturgical music. It inherently sounds more Western. Like Fr. Gregory, I do not render the original melodies exactly. I want them to be familiar but not exact, so as to transcend the original lyrics and become vehicles for the ancient liturgical texts. With that in mind, I sometimes place the melody in the alto line, and sometimes in the tenor.

---

* A note to musicians: Fr. Gregory's composition is in the fifth [plagal first] mode, one of the four diatonic modes.

More for Musicians

In the Russian-heritage choral tradition, it is common to have the top vocal line develop in parallel thirds above the melody, especially for two-part singing. In four-part arrangements, sometimes the melody falls in the tenor voice in Orthodox hymns. The device of placing the melody in the alto or tenor voice, rather than the soprano, contrasts with what Fr. Gregory did, putting the melody itself into a different "mode." In my compositions, when one or two voices float above the melody, they create new melodies in parallel with, or creating counterpoint to, the original—but in a different "mode." This cradles the original melody, leaving it discoverable, but not dominant. I believe, that by doing this, the composition becomes more hospitable to the new text as the fulfillment of the original.

In terms of building harmonies, I have approached this from different angles. Sometimes I develop each voice as a melody complete unto itself, resolving awkward places when the parts come together. At other times I focus on the original Spiritual melody, using the other vocal parts primarily for their chord function. An important factor, as I mentioned above, is whether or not the melody develops in a conjunct or disjunct manner; that is, stepwise and flowing, or with expanded chords or arpeggios.

Most of the Spirituals that I have arranged liturgically, use some expanded chords. In listening for what accompaniment the melody "wants," I find it often requires open fifths and fourths,* parallel fifths and octaves, and other features that are discouraged in classical Western music theory. Other composers have also found this to be the case when arranging Sacred Harp melodies.

Here is an interesting sidelight on Sacred Harp singing: It was also adopted in some African American parishes after emancipation, and is still sung today. A prominent feature of Sacred Harp is the use of the pentatonic scale.† Theodore F. Seward, who wrote down the Spirituals which formed Fisk Jubilee Singers' repertory in the 1800s, states that it is

> worthy of note that more than half the melodies in this connection are in the same scale as that in which Scottish

---

* A standard major chord: C-E-G. A standard minor chord: C-Eb-G. An open 5th: C-G. And an open 4th: C-F. These are neither major nor minor.

† A major pentatonic scale: C-D-E-G-A—the IV and the VII tones are missing.

music is written; that is, with the fourth and seventh tones omitted. The fact that the music of the ancient Greeks is also said to have been written in this scale suggests an interesting inquiry as to whether it may not be a peculiar language of nature, or a simpler alphabet than the ordinary diatonic scale,* in which the uncultivated mind finds its easiest expression.[2]

This tells us that composers who use the pentatonic scale to invoke an "American" feeling, based on Appalachian Sacred Harp, are creating something that very much includes African American heritage, although contemporary black people may not recognize it as such.

LET'S MOVE NOW from considerations of melody and harmony to considerations of how the music and text fit together. It is very important when composing and adapting Orthodox music for the music to accent stressed syllables.† In my work, this sometimes means that the notes may be identical in pitch and sometimes in duration but shift where they line up in their respective measures. Here is an example of the transformation from "Balm in Gilead":

into the "Our Father":

---

* A diatonic scale has seven notes—our standard major and minor scales.
† Hieromonk Andrew Wermuth discusses this in the context of how hymns are translated.

More for Musicians

So, as you can see in this example, the pitches are identical for each note in the phrases "There is a balm in" and in "Our Father, Who." But the duration of the notes, and how they fall in their respective measures is different. The rest of the melodic phrase in the "Our Father" is more interpretive.

This adaptation both changes the original melody, and at the same time leaves it recognizable. This is what I am looking for. As we have all experienced with amateur parish choirs, the words are often difficult to distinguish, and listeners depend on memory or books to follow along. So if the original melody is too dominant, the listeners' memory may substitute those lyrics for the liturgical prayer being sung, and, thus, the music's goal of adorning the prayer is defeated.

✤ ✤ ✤

IN MY POLYELEOS, I took the slow and mournful melody of "I Couldn't Hear Nobody Pray," (Fisk version) and sped it up, removing the blue notes.* Thus, this lamentation:

at twice the speed, becomes this hymn of praise:

---

* Blue notes are flatted third, fifth, or seventh tones; and sometimes semitones.

More for Musicians

In this key, the range of the melody goes too low for the sopranos (and too high for the tenors if transposed up). To prevent the sopranos from going down to a "B" on the final "alleluia," and to prevent having to write an even lower alto harmony, I shift the melody to the alto in these last three measures and whenever the refrain occurs.

Other Musical Considerations

HERE ARE SOME other musical considerations: One common feature of the Spirituals is call and response. This means that a song leader will call out a short phrase—sometimes it's a scripted part of the song, and sometimes it's spontaneous. Then the chorus answers with a short phrase of music, often a repeated chorus. This is reminiscent of two Orthodox liturgical features—the litany by the priest or deacon with the response by the congregation, and also antiphonal singing. I bring call and response into my Polyeleos by having the tenors and basses sing "Praise Him!" between the psalm verses and the "Alleluias." "Hallelu Jah" means "praise Jah," so "Praise Him!" is not actually an addition to the hymn, but rather a dynamic translation of the word "alleluia."

Another common feature of the Spirituals is short, rhythmic musical phrases. When adapting them for Orthodox liturgical usage, this poses one of the greatest challenges. When do I adapt the words to the music and when do I adapt the music to the words? What this really boils down to is which translation of the prayer to use, whether to use elements of different translations, or whether to create a new translation. This is something other composers and adapters also wrestle with.* In the "Our Father," I chose "debts" over "trespasses" out of metric considerations. In composing for such an iconic prayer, if the chosen melody required more adaptation of the words, I believe it would be time to try other melodies.

---

* See Hieromonk Andrew's article, p. 103.

> *More for Musicians*
>
> On the other hand, for the Polyeleos, I consulted three or four translations plus the Greek Psalter for wording. This was in addition to adapting the music to the text in every section. For "It is Truly Meet" —the hymn to the Mother of God that concludes the Anaphora—I had to make a decision about the phrase "more glorious beyond compare than the seraphim." The wording does not reflect the simple ethos of Spiritual music, and in forcing it into the cadence of the music, the wrong syllables would be accented. I ultimately used "and beyond compare outshining the seraphim in glory, glory, glory." Some people appreciate hearing a prayer phrase in different translation—it aids them to hear it more consciously; others find this to be a distraction.

Spirituals or Gospel Music?

SOME COMPOSERS are interested in creating liturgical music using Gospel music as their inspiration. And some wonder which will speak more deeply to the heart of African Americans—Spirituals or Gospel? And how would these approaches differ? In the chart below are some musical features that come to mind for me. Obviously, some of these are tendencies, not hard and fast rules.

Musical features	Spirituals	Gospel music
Anonymous folk music	✓	
Known composers (copyrights)		✓
Expanded melodic progression	✓	
Stepwise melodic progression		✓
Originally sung with harmony		✓
Incorporates jazz harmonies		✓
Short rhythmic phrasing	✓	✓
Call and response	✓	✓
Blue notes	✓	✓
Originally used instruments		✓

As I reflect on their similarities and differences, here's what stands out. Spirituals, by virtue of not having native Western harmonies, are easier to harmonize in a way that sounds both Western and Orthodox. Part of what is distinctive about Gospel is a familiar sound of their harmonies and chord progressions. It would be more challenging, in that case, to create a synthesis of style. On the other hand, some parishes, especially urban mission parishes, might want that unadulterated Gospel sound. Liturgical music needs to "sound like church" to the clergy and congregation of each unique parish.

Not all Gospel music uses instruments, of course—some is *a cappella*. But would Orthodox liturgical music based on Gospel potentially introduce a keyboard into the services? In the mid-twentieth century, there was a movement to inculturate Orthodox churches to a Western esthetic—this included architecture, use of stained-glass windows, and the introduction of pews and organs. So the use of keyboards would not be unprecedented, even though the long tradition of *a cappella* singing has a compelling theology.* It has helped generations of spiritual ancestors to "sing their way to heaven," to borrow Fr. Moses's phrase.

New Liturgical Texts

THERE HAVE BEEN times of prolific writing of liturgical (and para-liturgical texts), and times when writing was relatively stagnant. In the 18th century Russian Church, there was a flowering of the writing of akathists, inspired by the original one composed in honor of the Theotokos. As new saints are glorified here and abroad, there have been opportunities to write liturgical hymns and services in their honor. For example, there is the service with an akathist to St. Nikolai Velimirović, written by Mother Macaria Corbett.[3] Finding inspiration in various places, Dr. Carla Thomas has written the

---

* The theological argument for *a cappella* singing in the Orthodox Church is that all sounds should be "rational," that is, expressing words.

"Canon for Racial Reconciliation"* as well as a "Canon to All Saints of Africa." Most recently, in July of 2021, the Fellowship of St. Moses the Black published the *Akathist to the Merciful Savior: Healer of the Wounds of American Slavery*.[4] This akathist was published under the authorship of the Fellowship itself. I hesitated to put my name to it, but Fr. Moses said that I need to "for the sake of history," and I can see his point.

Speaking of akathists, what exactly are they? An akathist is a lengthy prayer poem, of 12 sections, usually sung in praise of the Theotokos Mary, our Lord, an event from their lives, or of saints or angels. Each section is composed of two stanzas. The first stanza is called a "kontakion," which ends in a thrice sung "alleluia." The second stanza is called an "ikos," which is usually followed by several couplets of praise to the saint or the occasion, ending in a common refrain.

This new akathist is written in praise of Christ Himself as the Merciful Savior. The "alleluias" are sung only in praise of Him. But the "kontakia" and "ikoi" are sung in praise of martyrs and confessors in the American lands. Which martyrs and confessors? Orthodoxy came here with little, if any, of the bloodshed which was so integral to the spread of the Early Church. Martyrs—a word which comes from the Greek for "witnesses"—are those who testify to the truth of Christ with their blood. They embraced bodily death for Christ rather than the spiritual death of renouncing their faith. Confessors suffered for their faith without explicitly dying for it. Thus, it appears impossible for our soil to have been enriched by the blood of holy martyrs and confessors as it has in historically Orthodox locations.

In fact, however, we are rich in martyrs and confessors. They are the enslaved Africans who, contrary to the popular myth that evangelism "justified" enslavement, were often forbidden to pray or worship, either by those with immediate control over their bodies or by local statute. Fr. Paul

---

* See Appendix I of this volume, p. 179.

Abernathy demonstrates in his new book, *The Prayer of a Broken Heart,*[5] that while many of the enslaved were introduced to the Christian Faith during the time of the Great Awakening, a number actually came to Christ, not by catechism, but by a direct revelation to their inward being.

Sojourner Truth was one such soul. She had nothing in mind but an upcoming slave holiday when she was struck by a vision of God. At first she was terrified, sensing His transcendent holiness and her small sinfulness. This was followed by a reassuring vision of Christ and His love for her. Others, who had no access to reading the Bible, found that the Holy Spirit placed the scriptures in their hearts, as happened with St. Mary of Egypt in the sixth century.

The Psalmist David says "God is wonderful in His pious ones; the God of Israel, He will give power and strength unto His people. Blessed be God" (Ps 67:35 LXX). God works wonderful things through those who dedicate their lives to Him. It is the activity of the Holy Spirit that empowers them to triumph over temptations and torments, and to face martyrdom with their eye single on God. Thus, in praising His pious ones, we are praising Him, too. Therefore, our new akathist praises the martyrs who, we know, were killed explicitly for refusing to deny Christ or to stop praying. We also praise the heroic exploits of those who suffered abuse for Christ's sake. Perhaps we only know one episode from a life. But we praise righteousness wherever we see it; in doing so, we are praising God Himself.

Regarding the form of this akathist, instead of each "ikos" having the customary succession of praise couplets, there is one final refrain which encapsulates the whole work:

Remember, O Merciful Savior, the souls of those
who died in bitter bondage,
And hear the intercessions of Thine American Saints
both known and unknown.

Thus, we humbly pray for the repose of those souls whose unrequited labors helped build up Western nations. To paraphrase St. Paul, we are their material beneficiaries; shall we not labor a little for their spiritual benefit in return? (see Rom 15:27). Conversely in our own spiritual poverty, we ask for the intercession of those who are saints in God's eyes. Divine Mercy knows who they are—just as when we sing the annual commemoration to All Saints. The Church has long recognized that many saints are known to God alone, and has provided ways for us to honor the hidden ones. Because of the mysterious connection between the living and the departed, we believe that the Akathist to the Merciful Savior is an ideal vehicle to pray for peace and reconciliation in our land.

Parting Thoughts and Hopes

WHEN I BEGAN this reflection two years ago, I had not yet met Dr. Zhanna Lehmann, the choir conductor who has been bringing my compositions to light. I had not yet had the privilege of interviewing Orthodox liturgical composers Benedict Sheehan or nazo zakkak for the "Postscript" above.* These happy meetings have greatly broadened the horizon of my hopes.

I hope, among other blessings, for a flowering of prayer and hymn composition, here in the Americas, that will open a door of hospitality into the Orthodox Faith for people of African descent. There is room for pious poets to amplify the praises of our righteous ones. There is room for historians to shed more light on godly lives, brave lives, otherworldly lives. There is room for iconographers … .

I was motivated to share my compositional journey in hopes of inspiring and encouraging other composers. Now it appears that the Holy Spirit is, Himself, already recruiting people to this much-needed work. And so now I rejoice in the hope of mutual inspiration and fruitful collaboration among liturgical composers, as well as for the raising up of new ones.

---

* See p. 122.

I hope for children to say, "I could grow up to write songs for the Church." There are many stones still unturned, many possibilities for drawing from the wellspring of Spirituals and Gospel music. However this work develops, I hope that in time all peoples may hear in their own musical language the mighty works of God (see Acts 2:11).

III
FROM THE FIELD

10

THE
VOICE
OF
THE HEART

DR. ZHANNA LEHMANN

Beginnings: Music and Faith

M USIC HAS PLAYED an essential role my entire life and I will share how music brought me to, and sustains me in my faith in Jesus Christ, and the surprising part played by African American Spirituals. The regeneration of religious activity—including both the reopening and renovation of churches and monasteries in Russia in the last decade of the 20th century—was a response to the decades of atheism and persecution of Christians in the Soviet Union, mandated by the state. This period saw increased church attendance and new interest in the use of spiritual themes in the cinema, literature, and music. The churches and cathedrals also experienced the need for choirs to serve numerous services for the increased attendance. The tradition for churches to have choirs consisting of well-trained musicians was revived, and it brought many professional musicians of diverse backgrounds and training, music-major students, music teachers, and other well-trained musicians to seek employment in the Orthodox temples. Whether they were followers of the Faith or not, they were welcomed if they could sing on a professional level.

It was during this regeneration that I was baptized and became a follower of the Russian Orthodox Church. I was eager to read as many books as I could about Christian history, the saints, and theology. While at the Music Conservatory in Kazan, Russia, I was a student in its Choral Conducting department and was blessed to get a coveted position as a member of the choir at St. Nicholas Church in Kazan. During this time, I participated literally in all the services offered in the church, sometimes singing more than once a day. During the Paschal season one year, I sang so many services that I lost my voice. Because of my participation in the church choir, I began attending church on a regular basis. Through my singing in the choir and my increased attendance at church, I became a more devout Christian and developed an intimate understanding of the music of the church services.

Years later, after becoming a member of St. Nicholas Antiochian Orthodox Church in Champaign-Urbana, Illinois, I found out that St. Raphael of Brooklyn—the head of the Antiochian Mission in the beginning of the 20th century, and the first Orthodox Christian bishop of North America—had lived and taught at the Kazan Theological Seminary! We lived and served God in the same city a hundred years apart. Another interesting and astonishing fact in my life is that the milestones of my path as a Christian have been always connected with churches named after St. Nicholas. Those churches are in different cities and countries, but all under the patronage of St. Nicholas.

During my five years of graduate studies at the Kazan State Conservatory, I was a member of an upper-level, elite choir with a very intense schedule of rehearsals and performance preparations. The choir met six days a week, for practice sessions of a minimum of three hours each day. A famous Russian conductor and choir master directed this ensemble—Professor Semen Kazachkov (1909–2005), who was known for his excellent choirs and their performances throughout Russia.* Prof. Kazachkov taught his students comprehensive and polystylistic techniques for conducting and directing the choir. This means that the choice of techniques for conducting and singing depends on a close examination of the style of the composition, a detailed theoretical analysis of it, and intuitive following of the inner hearing of the piece. As a member of this choir, I was introduced to all different genres of choir music including Western classical music, Russian folk and classical music, and the African American Spirituals. Out of all the genres that I sang and performed with this choir, the Spirituals impacted me strongly, and in a different way than the other styles. Among the first Spirituals that we performed were "Soon I Will Be Done" (I still have a handwritten copy of it in my personal library!), "Deep River," "Joshua Fit the Battle of Jericho," "My Lord, What a Morning,"† and "Swing Low, Sweet Chariot."

As a musician, I was impressed with the inner energy and strength that came from the melodies and words of the Spirituals. They created a feeling of sadness and sorrow that affected one's spirit and soul, and I felt that only an accomplished vocalist or singer could perform this type of music in order to convey those feelings to the audience.

Having no experience singing this genre, and having never even heard any songs of this type before, we sang the pieces in the manner of classical music, rather than an authentic style. It would only be later, when I moved to the United States, that I heard the music of the African American Spirituals sung in the

---

* He was a student of the other famous conductors, V. Stepanov (1890–1954) and I. Musin (1903/04–1999), who were professors at St. Petersburg Conservatory.

† *Editor's footnote:* This is alternately rendered "My Lord, What a Mourning." Because of the oral/aural tradition of the African American Spirituals, both spellings and meanings are attested to, starting with the earliest published collections.

style and manner that they were meant to be performed. Only then did I come to realize the true potential of this genre, both as a style that can evoke strong personal feelings and responses, and as a style that can have a deep religious meaning, that can bring people closer to God.

The question one may ask is how this music captures the Russian audience and what attracts both professional and amateur choirs in Russia to include the American Spirituals in their repertoire. At first glance, Spirituals seem to be so distant from the traditional styles of Russian vocal music—folk, secular, or sacred—but upon closer examination one can trace some similarities between Spirituals and such genres of Russian music as folk songs and "Spiritual poems," which I will discuss below.

In Russian folk music, the melody plays the predominant role, with a soloist initiating the melodic line. Then other voices join to create a unique polyphonic texture and harmonic structures. There are many possibilities for generating these harmonies. A few possible variants are when each voice leads its own line, and the harmonies arise as an interrelation of these independent lines; the other method is when the voices subordinate and harmonize the main melody. Spirituals, representing a significant form of the American folksong, also typically have a leader that shouts and initiates a hymn in an improvisational manner to which a chorus responds. Most often, both Russian folk songs and Spirituals are sung *a cappella*.

Spirituals appeared for many purposes, including the expression of religious or ceremonial ideas. In Russian folk tradition there is a unique genre that is named the "Penitential" psalms or poems, comprised of a mix of old Russian lyrical poetry, religious ideas, and the minstrel practice of street entertainment. This minstrelsy first appeared in the second half of the 15th century, and was actively developed through the 17th century. These Penitential poems form part of a larger poetic genre collectively known as "Spiritual poems," mentioned above. The traveling minstrels, called *kaliki* or *kaleki*, made a living by singing Spiritual poems in public market squares. They attended the church services and absorbed the styles of chanting and singing they heard there into their own performances. The *kaliki* also made pilgrimages to the Holy Land and other spiritual places. As a result of their pilgrimages, the *kaliki* synthesized Palestinian and Byzantine traditions, which then were infused into their native culture. Their expressive and emotional singing on the Christian themes of repentance, the Last Judgement, and the Theotokos moved the crowds to tears. The Penitential poems became a powerful way of communicating the knowledge of Christian ideas to the broader population and a diverse secular audience. When the Penitential poems emerged from the monasteries and the Orthodox literary tradition, they assimilated folkloric practices, which came to define their essence. One can draw an analogy between this type of preaching on biblical and Christian themes, in their own unique musical style performed outside of churches, with the American Spirituals, which also drew their thematic inspiration from the Bible (the psalms, narratives etc.). Neither the Russian Spiritual poems or the American Spirituals used the biblical material literally, but it was creatively interpreted by singers, who altered the text and melodies, bringing out the symbolic aspect of the biblical themes, and expressing it through the prism of their own life experience. While the major body of the Russian Spiritual poems was developed by the end of the 17th century, this time marked the conception of the African American Spiritual genre. The enslaved Africans came from different places but they brought some common singing practices which initiated the emergence of the Spirituals in later times.

One musical aspect of the Spirituals, that makes them attractive for choirs, comes from their great liveliness and energy. The presence of dance rhythms, which readily inspire singers to move in a musical unity, underline freedom of dynamic improvisations. Another aspect is their almost natural demand for powerful voices to provide the energetic lead for a group of singers. The singing of Spirituals awakens the voice of the heart. Spirituals also have the incredible ability to touch the heart of listeners and let them feel the joy of the religious experience in their souls.

That first experience in Russia of being a singer in the church choir as well as a singer of a high-level choir in the Conservatory provided me with a diversified experience which I appreciated years later, when I took on different roles serving the Church in the US. I became a regent for the Russian-language services at Three Hierarchs Greek Orthodox Church in Champaign-Urbana; these were served once a month by a visiting priest for the local Russian community. Subsequently, I became a chanter and choir director at St. Nicholas Antiochian Orthodox Church in Urbana. That first intense experience in Russia was like a concentrated essence of the multiple skills and knowledge that I would later need, distilled to a high concentration. Through the years I have been taking a drop of this precious elixir, to which I add my new experiences, developed from achievements and mistakes alike. I flavor it with new knowledge received and learned from remarkable people that I meet; my cup for drinking in God's wisdom never empties, but is always full.

American Liturgical Music

My PERSONAL EXPERIENCE with American liturgical music began around the year 2012 when I became a chanter at St. Nicholas Orthodox Church in Urbana-Champaign. At that time, I was also working on my Doctorate degree in Choral Music at the University of Illinois. I had to conduct a recital as a partial fulfillment of the degree. The requirement for the recital was to prepare a performance of choral works for a chorus and instrumental ensemble from all periods of music history. All the pieces that I selected for my recital were on the theme of Christian music. One of the pieces that I chose to represent the contemporary period of the 21st century was a choral work by a contemporary American Orthodox composer.

During the years of being involved in the academic environment and participating in university choirs as well as in a few local community choirs, I was dreaming about my own choir that would sing Orthodox music. After a few years of attempting to find enthusiasts who would support my idea, things worked out at St. Nicholas Church in Urbana, and in 2015, the Illinois Orthodox Choir came into existence. This pan-Orthodox vocal group is comprised of singers from the Vermilion and Champaign counties. The Illinois Orthodox Choir celebrates and performs Orthodox Christian music of all nations and a bit of other Christian music. As both the director of the St. Nicholas choir and the director of a community choir—which actively performs and "preaches" the Orthodox Faith through music to various audiences—I continuously look for new pieces to add into our repertoire. I am certainly interested in contemporary Orthodox compositions since their music language and compositional style will speak to present-day listeners.

The other source for enriching my knowledge of American Orthodox composers has been the conferences I regularly attend. Among them are the International Society for Orthodox Church Musicians and the Sacred Music Institute of the Antiochian Archdiocese of North America. I met some of the contemporary composers in person at those conferences and I was delighted to participate in discussions about the state of the Orthodox music in the US.

The Orthodox music of the last decades in the US and other countries is multifaceted and complex due to the wide range of their stylistic characteristics and the variety of the compositional techniques that the composers utilize. I will mention only a few of the many noteworthy methods that modern Orthodox composers employ. These techniques include a synthesis of styles; the quotation and adaption of melodies from instrumental genres and works of other composers; an application of a technique known as an allusion. In a musical allusion, the composer doesn't incorporate a style of music directly but partially applies stylistic elements to create associations and subtle hints of that style. Another compositional method is the incorporation of music from non-Orthodox religious cultures.

With the technique of adaption, mentioned above, a composer reworks and adapts a melody of an instrumental piece (often a well-known one) into a vocal composition, setting the Orthodox liturgical text to this melody. Musical instruments are traditionally not permitted in the Orthodox services; thus, a fresh vocal interpretation of an instrumental piece gives it a new meaning and function at the liturgical services.

The method of using music from non-Orthodox religious cultures in Orthodox compositions bridges various religious and cultural spheres, giving the music exposure to a broader audience outside of its native environment. A no less important effect of this musical assimilation is the warm acceptance of this style by the Orthodox Christian converts from the diverse range of religious or non-religious backgrounds in the US. According to the Assembly of Canonical Orthodox Bishops of the United States of America, by 2015, almost half of the current number of Orthodox Christians here were converts. The new compositions, utilizing stylistic elements of music that is more familiar to the American congregation and that has "an American flavor," encourages more congregational participation in the singing during the Liturgy. The result of this is that some congregations have begun using these pieces within their services in preference to the more traditional, classical pieces.

When a friend of mine* asked me if I would be interested in looking at music compositions by Mother Katherine (Weston) and to consider performing them with the Illinois Orthodox Choir, which I direct, I saw it as a unique opportunity

---

* *Editor's footnote:* This friend is Molly Sanderson, a music teacher who earned her MM (Master's degree in Music) from the University of Illinois at Champaign-Urbana. She is the older daughter of Fr. Jerome Sanderson: founding member, regular conference presenter, and former Vice President of the Fellowship of St. Moses the Black.

to perform a type of music that no one has done before—a synthesis of the traditional American Spiritual with Orthodox music. I have been honored and humbled to direct the premiere of four choral pieces by Mother Katherine: the Cherubic Hymn ("Sometimes I Feel Like a Motherless Child"), "It is Right Indeed" ("Were You There When They Crucified My Lord?"), the "Our Father" ("Balm in Gilead"), and the Polyeleos ("I Couldn't Hear Nobody Pray").

Later, when the choir at my church first sang Mother Katherine's Cherubic Hymn during the Divine Liturgy, it was met with a respectful hush. The people were awed by the music and became more attentive to the message communicated through it. One of the altar servers commented that the music created a "heavenly moment" in the worship service and space—that moment when earth meets heaven … a moment of sacred mystery. A few weeks earlier, we had done a concert performance of the same piece. Hearing God's message delivered through the energy of the music, people were caught up in the moment, their eyes welling up with tears. At the rehearsal, I had encouraged the choir members to sing Mother Katherine's pieces, not by their external voice but by the voice of their hearts.

Subsequently, in July of 2022, I had the opportunity to present the same Cherubic Hymn during a plenary session of the above-mentioned Sacred Music Institute at the Antiochian Village in Pennsylvania. After my introductory remarks, I conducted approximately 80 voices in singing the hymn. It was warmly received and participants were pleasantly surprised by the unique sound and the experience as a whole. Spirituals emphasize the voice of the singers as a manifestation of the strength of their soul. It awakens our hearts and opens our souls to receive the heavenly message from God about His kingdom and the road to our salvation through His words.

Mother Katherine's music includes all the characteristics described above. Furthermore, her music is appealing to me for her thorough approach to setting the Orthodox text to the melodies of the original African American Spirituals and aligning the context of the initial text of the Spiritual to the new liturgical purpose of the Orthodox service. Her treatment of melodic lines, preserving the emotional context of the original melodies, and the precise and pure harmonies amaze me with their beauty. The compositions by Mother Katherine are feasible for a medium size choir of church singers with a basic music training.

I find great joy in working with Mother Katherine, assisting her in editing the scores from my experience as a conductor, singer, and music theory teacher. The challenge for me as a classically trained musician and an experienced conductor of Russian sacred choral music, is how to preserve the unique musical features that distinguish the music of the African American Spirituals and to synthesize them into the classical model of four-part vocal harmony, which is a traditional attribute of choral singing in the Orthodox Church.

Spirituals have at their heart the soulful lyric, dedicated to God; through choral singing they generate a highly creative expression and heartfelt performance. This energetically and emotionally powerful music, incorporated into the Orthodox services through carefully considered choices, will conquer the hearts of church singers and the faithful, and will become an excellent resource for the practice of our faith.

11

THE SPIRIT OF ORTHODOXY CHOIR
REFLECTIONS ON SINGING ARRANGEMENTS FROM SPIRITUALS
STRATOS MANDALAKIS

Editor's Note: Stratos Mandalakis and I were given an email intro-
duction by Dr. Zhanna Lehmann. He shared with me the history
and vision of the Spirit of Orthodoxy Choir, as well as videos of per-
formances. When he expressed interest in adding my pieces based on
Spirituals to their repertoire, I was genuinely interested to hear from
the director of a long-established Orthodox choir, how these pieces
would fit into their ethos and vision. After all, it's about evangelism,
and about those who come after. In response, he kindly sent this con-
tribution for Jubilation.

T HE SPIRIT OF ORTHODOXY CHOIR, as an inter-jurisdic-
tional choir, has prided itself in bringing to its audiences
the classics of the Slavic repertoire along with settings from
the Greek, Antiochian, Serbian, Ukrainian, Georgian traditions, chants in the various forms, and music arranged and
composed by living Orthodox Christian composers here and
abroad. We sing the majority of our selections in English and

strive to bring the beauty of Orthodoxy from both the Byzantine and Western liturgical traditions to our audiences.

It is a blessing to have learned of the beautiful hymn arrangements done by Mother Katherine, and having African American musical roots. How better to reach Americans than by using a musical genre that is part of the fabric of our culture! For if we look at how Orthodox Christian music has evolved and developed, it is obvious that the musical settings never develop in a vacuum.

In the early Church, Jewish and Gregorian chants for the same psalm are known to be identical, as the Church borrowed directly from the melodies used in temple worship that preceded it. The Trisagion Prayer is used in the Latin Rite on Holy Friday and is traditionally sung in Greek and Latin (along with English in the Anglican Liturgy).

Early Slavic chant forms have their basis in the Byzantine chant prevalent before and after the first millennium, and it is even easy to hear similarities in early Slavic, Byzantine, and some Gregorian chants of the same mode. The received tradition of modern Byzantine chant has been greatly influenced by music of the Ottoman Empire. Exposure to Western choral traditions has influenced Slavic choral music for several centuries and Greek Orthodox Church chant melodies have been arranged in Western choral styles that even utilize an organ ... again ... music is not created in a vacuum!

In America, if we are going to attract people from all walks of life we will need to worship using music that more reflects the culture in which we are surrounded. Our liturgical music is called to bring us joy—a certain joyful sobriety that is the essence of the Orthodox Christian way of life. Dance or pop music can often make us happy for a fleeting moment, but this kind of emotionally charged music does not fit the bill. ... I like to think of the word "hagiography" (which is the biography of a saint) when thinking about the melodies we must use because the Greek word "hagios" or holy, literally means not earthly ... in other words ... "we need to be composing something out of this world"... our melodies need to be holy/otherworldly for we are actually joining the eternal choirs of angels singing to God's glory when we sing in worship! St. John Chrysostom describes this:

> Above, the armies of angels praise while below the people are standing in the choir of the church and imitating their praise. The Seraphim above cry the thrice-holy hymn and the people below raise the same hymn.[1]

And we in America are surrounded by melodies that can bring us to this joyous, this out-of-this-world experience! Gospel, soulful jazz, revivalist hymns, Appalachian folk tunes, shape note hymns, Spirituals ... all of these musical genres contain in them many of the same musical and modal characteristics inherent in our church music from the past. And because of that these more contemporary genres can bring us to that state of otherworldliness that St. Vladimir's emissaries experienced in Hagia Sophia where they "knew not whether they were on earth or in heaven, but were convinced that if God dwelt anywhere it was in there."

All of us know that hearing/singing "Amazing Grace," "Beautiful Star of Bethlehem," "Simple Gifts," "Swing Low Sweet Chariot," or "Were You There When They Crucified My Lord," surely stirs our souls the same way we are stirred by Bortniansky's, Kastalsky's, Glagolev's or Sander's free composed pieces, or Obikhod, Kievan, Znamenny, Georgian or Byzantine chant.

As St. John Chrysostom said:

> Nothing so uplifts the mind, giving it wings and freeing it from the earth, releasing it from the prison of the body, affecting it with love of wisdom, and causing it to scorn all things pertaining to this life, as modulated melody and the divine chant.[2]

Knowing that our Orthodox music today is *nothing* like what Chrysostom heard in the Church during his life—for it didn't yet exist—we have to believe that modulating or changing melodies drawn from the more indigenous American musical styles will uplift our minds, giving them wings—and will do the same for seekers who are more familiar with these American genres.

Mother Katherine, we look forward to learning and are excited about programming these and future settings that come from your hand. May God grant you many years and may Christ have mercy on you and give you the strength and wisdom to continue this work through the prayers of St. John of Damascus, St. Kassiane the Hymnographer, St. Romanos the Melodist, St. John Koukouzeles, the Theotokos and all the Saints! Amen.

12

RECONCILIATION
PRAYER
IN THE
OPEN AIR

MIKHAIL MARKHASEV

Editor's Note: The following introduction has been provided by a member of the Orthodox Christian Prison Ministry with the help and approval of the author:

MIKHAIL MARKHASEV was born in Ukraine to parents of Ukrainian and Russian descent. He and his family fled Ukraine in the late 1980s, as the Soviet Union began to crumble, and landed in Southern California. Feeling alienated as a young immigrant and confused about his identity (Orthodox Christian on his mother's side, Jewish on his father's), Mikhail eventually found acceptance and validation in a Mexican gang. He is now serving life without parole at Corcoran State Prison in California for committing murder during a roadside robbery gone awry.

While imprisoned at Corcoran, Mikhail encountered the concept of restorative justice and mercy through the Victim Impact Statements submitted during his sentencing. Mikhail's victim's family asked the court to spare his life, not wanting to inflict on his family the same pain and suffering Mikhail had inflicted on theirs. It was only then, after many years in prison, that Mikhail began to repent of his crimes. He publicly acknowledged his guilt, dropped all of his legal appeals, left his prison gang, and embraced the Christ of the Gospels and the Orthodox Church.

Today, Mikhail is devoted to a life of prayer, study, and service to other inmates of different races, tutoring them in classwork, and encouraging them in the faith. He is godfather to a former inmate and fellow gang-dropout who embraced St. Moses the Black as his patron saint when he was baptized and chrismated in the Orthodox Church. Now let us hear from Mikhail in his own words.

RECONCILIATION PRAYER IN THE OPEN AIR

LIKE A MENACING CONSTRICTOR, the COVID-19 restrictions squeezed us out of our chapel services, so we had to take our Vespers to the yard. It was crowded, but the brother and I stood at the edge, beneath the gun tower (which became our makeshift cupola), with the evening sun glistening in the barbed wire of the perimeter fence. Facing east with a sprawling field before us, we quietly chanted the "Canon for Racial Reconciliation," which was written by a member of the Orthodox Christian Prison Ministry (OCPM) board of trustees* and provided to us by a friend who is also involved with OCPM.

Under the "cupola" stand two recovering racists, both of whom are serving life in prison for murdering persons of other races ... . It may seem odd to hear that we pray such a Canon in a place rife with racial divisions, regional cliques, and gang affiliation. But this is God's doing in Christ, who "is our peace, who has made both one, and has broken down the middle wall of separation, having abolished in His flesh the

---

* Dr. Carla Thomas.

enmity" (Eph 2:14–15). This is how God is pleased to work in the place of our exile and punishment, where we are granted repentance and are commanded to "bear fruits worthy of repentance" (Lk 3:8).

And if this means demolishing the satanic strongholds of our sinful past by saturating the atmosphere with prayer for racial reconciliation—the atmosphere, thick with cursing, complaining, and blasphemy—then here is another token of Christ's resurrecting power. Even more, when we praise God "for all the flowers in His garden"* as we journey back to our Father's house—through the sin-soiled wilderness which has seen so much hostility and hatred—we are also praying for those around us, asking the Lord to "close all the loftily divisive and distracting worldly windows, and bring us to the doors of repentance."†

---

* This and the following excerpt are taken from the "Canon for Racial Reconciliation." See Appendix I for the full text of the canon.
† Sessional hymn (sedalion) after the third ode.

APPENDICES

APPENDIX I

CANON
FOR RACIAL
RECONCILIATION

DR. CARLA THOMAS

Tone 2

Ode I

Irmos: In the deep of old, the infinite power / overwhelmed Pharaoh's whole army, / but the incarnate Word annihilated pernicious sin, / exceedingly glorious is the Lord, / for gloriously hath He been glorified.

Glory to God for all the flowers in His garden.

Because "the Stone which the builders refused is become the head stone of the corner,"* the disparate races are conjoined again.

Glory to the Father, and to the Son, and to the Holy Spirit.

Even as Christ commanded us to love the Lord our God with all our heart, and with all our soul, and with all our mind,

---

* Ps 118:22

and with all our strength,* so He also called us to love our neighbor as ourselves.†

Both now and ever, and to the ages of ages. Amen.

The sum of humanity's reconciliation to God is voiced in one acclamation: O Most-pure one, thou art the Theotokos, she who bears God.

Ode III

Irmos: By establishing me on the rock of faith, / Thou hast enlarged my mouth over my enemies, / and my spirit rejoices when I sing: / There is none holy as our God, / and none righteous beside Thee, O Lord.

Glory to God for all the flowers in His garden.

Putting behind Noah's curse,‡ we press "toward the mark for the prize of the high calling of God in Christ Jesus,"§ by seeing the mark of God's creative hand upon each face.

Glory to the Father, and to the Son, and to the Holy Spirit.

Splintered by callous condemnation, Noah's sons split the races in three. But the blood of the Second Person of the Trinity filled the divide, restoring a common humanity in Christ.

Both now and ever, and to the ages of ages. Amen.

Most-holy Theotokos, not only hast thou joined man to God but thou hast also begun the process of reconciling man to man and race to race.

Sedalion, Tone 4

O Lord, when Thou wilt close all the loftily divisive and distracting worldly windows, bring us to the doors of repentance.

---

* Mk 12:30

† Lev 19:18; Mt 19:19; Mt 22:39; Mk 12:31; cf. Lk 10:27; Rom 13:9; Gal 5:14 & Jas 2:8.

‡ Gen 9:25, 26

§ Phil 3:14

By the left door of remorse, let us bring our hearts, broken and humbled. By the right door of resolve, let us bring our minds wholly redirected by Thy Holy Spirit to Thy throne, O Christ. Bring us to that table where all may find a place. For all the races of humanity may be found in Thy garden, where each of us is one of Thy beloved flowers.

Glory to the Father, and to the Son, and to the Holy Spirit, both now and ever, and to the ages of ages. Amen.

Theotokion: All-holy Lady Theotokos, shield the eye of our heart from the distractions of this rebellious world. Be our guide in both contrition and godly resolve, so that we may be found worthy of that heavenly banquet where all may find a place. For all the races of humanity may be found in thy Son's garden, where each of us is one of His beloved flowers.

Ode IV

Irmos: From a Virgin didst Thou come, not as an ambassador nor as an angel, / but the very Lord himself incarnate, / and didst save me the whole man. / Wherefore I cry to Thee: / Glory to Thy power, O Lord.

Glory to God for all the flowers in His garden.

Putting behind the pain of his brother's murder, St. Dionysius brought forth fruits of repentance for his family. He applied the forgiving balm of Christ to the contrite soul of his brother's murderer. He gave him the sacrament of absolution after the man sincerely confessed his sins.

Glory to the Father, and to the Son, and to the Holy Spirit.

God in three Hypostases, Father, Son and Holy Spirit, regards the heart, not the might nor the melanin. Therefore, will I trust in Him who has made all things, sees all things, hears all things and feels all things, great and small.

Both now and ever, and to the ages of ages. Amen.

O compassionately loving Mary, full of grace and mercy, teach us to love one another, even when love is not initially returned.

Ode V

Irmos: Thou who art the light of those lying in darkness, / and the salvation of the despairing, O Christ my Savior, / I rise early to pray to Thee, O King of Peace. / Enlighten me with Thy radiance, / for I know no other God beside Thee.

Glory to God for all the flowers in His garden.

Putting behind the mark of Cain,* we strive to see past our neighbors' specks and concentrate on our own remarkably large logs of sin† that need unceasing prayer.

Glory to the Father, and to the Son, and to the Holy Spirit.

The consubstantial Trinity in God glorified seeks the restoration by adoption of all mankind. Yet all must come to the throne of grace by free will. How wonderful is our God.

Both now and ever, and to the ages of ages. Amen.

Sweet Mother of the Merciful God, thy raiment has threads from the four corners of the earth; wherefore all generations, everywhere, bless thee.‡

Ode VI

Irmos: Whirled about in the abyss of sin, / I appeal to the unfathomable abyss of Thy compassion: / from corruption raise me up, O God.

Glory to God for all the flowers in His garden.

Putting behind the memories of being sold into slavery, Joseph acknowledged that it was God and not his apologetic brothers who "did send me before you to preserve life."§ So also let us acknowledge the fulfillment of God's ineffable will.

---

* Gen 4:15
† Cf. Mt 7:3 & Lk 6:41
‡ See Lk 1:48
§ Gen 45:5

Glory to the Father, and to the Son, and to the Holy Spirit.

The Father, Son, and Holy Spirit are one in essence and undivided. Man, though created, has been granted everlasting salvation by partaking of the body and blood of Christ. Thus is man reunited to God and to man.

Both now and ever, and to the ages of ages. Amen.

Rejoice, O Virgin, for He who made thy womb more spacious than the heavens, has come through thee to reconcile man to God and man to man.

Kontakion, Tone 4

For the weak, let us share strength, and let the strong forego condemnation. For, in Christ, the strong can bear the infirmities of the weak; through Him all things can be done, for the Trinity alone is the Holy God, holy and strong, holy and immortal.

Ode VII

Irmos: When the golden image was worshipped in the plain of Dura, / Thy three children despised the godless order, / thrown into the fire, they were bedewed and sang: / blessed art Thou, O God of our fathers.

Glory to God for all the flowers in His garden.

As all races may build the bridge of reconciliation through a sharing of the fruits of repentance, so relationship is reformed. While the prodigal son shares the fruit of humility, the older brother offers the fruit of patience and forgiveness.*

Glory to the Father, and to the Son, and to the Holy Spirit.

Putting behind the cries of betrayal, Christ carried forward His cross. By love and obedience, not by nails, did He remain on the cross, trampling death by death.

---

* See Lk 15:11 ff

Both now and ever, and to the ages of ages. Amen.

Putting behind the crucifying cries, the Holy Virgin endured a pain worse than the travail of birth. By love, she gave birth to Love. By faith, she went from strength to strength. By hope, she watched the Light of Light slip into hades and then soar back to the heavens.

Ode VIII

Irmos: O ye works, praise the Lord God, who descended / into the fiery furnace with the Hebrew children / and changed the flame into dew, / and supremely exalt Him unto all ages.

Glory to God for all the flowers in His garden.

Putting behind the memories of Israel, Daniel kept his sight on God, though he was a stranger in a strange land.*

Glory to God for all the flowers in His garden.

Even as repentance is more than being sorry, so racial reconciliation is more than the giving and accepting of apologies. The fruit of repentance may vary in form and fashion: The Prophet David offered a psalm,† and Righteous Zacchaeus, a four-fold restoration;‡ St. John Maximovitch offered his prayer, fasting, and care for orphans.

Glory to the Father, and to the Son, and to the Holy Spirit.

In repentance, St. Menas offered his martyr's blood, and St. Luke, his icons and healing counsel; St. Herman left familiar surroundings to bring Orthodoxy to America; St. Thaïs offered her thankful, heartfelt, and tearful prayers; St. Moses offered his humble bag of spilling sand.

Both now and ever, and to the ages of ages. Amen.

O Mary, Joy of All Who Sorrow, sanctify us by thy intercession before thy Son and our Savior. For He, who sat upon

---

* Dan 1:1 ff

† Ps 50 (LXX)

‡ Lk 19:8

thy arm, is strong and mighty, True God of True God. Help us to reunite together in love, patient co-suffering and unspeakable joy.

Ode IX

Irmos: God the Word, who came forth from God, / and who by ineffable wisdom came to renew Adam after his grievous fall to corruption through eating, / and who ineffably took flesh from the Holy Virgin for our sake, / Him do we the faithful with one accord magnify with hymns.

Glory to God for all the flowers in His garden.

Putting behind the sorrow of racial division, let us see the good and commonality of one another in Christ, for the garment of gladness is the same.

Glory to the Father, and to the Son, and to the Holy Spirit.

Let God be glorified from above, and from united voices below. Let those with much share, so there would be none with little.* Let the daily loaves which the Lord sends be divided generously, so that the races will no longer be prone to division.

Both now and ever, and to the ages of ages. Amen.

Yea, Holy Mother, awesome reconciler who cannot be put to shame, help us to heal our wounds of race—and every human categorization—with the binding balm of the all-embracing Christ, who shall come again with glory, and whose manifold, united Kingdom will have no end.

Prayer

Holy and exalted Lord Jesus Christ, who hast made of one blood all the race of humankind,† and in whom "there is neither Jew nor Greek, there is neither bond nor free, there is

---

* Cf. 2 Cor 8:15

† See Act 17:26

neither male nor female";* who hast given us the saving commandment "Love thy neighbor as thyself";† we, Thy unworthy servants, praise and bless Thee who hast done all things for our salvation: Thy incarnation, baptism, and ministry; Thy passion, death, and resurrection; Thy holy ascension by which Thou hast brought our human nature to sit with the Father on the heavenly throne; and for sending Thy Comforter Spirit to teach us and guide us in all our ways: Free our hearts and minds from judgment of those who appear to be different from us, and teach us, rather, to delight in all the flowers in Thy garden. Let Thy peace, which passes all human understanding,‡ illuminate our hearts and shine forth into this rebellious world. And, O Lord Jesus Christ, make us worthy to be united with Thee and with one another in Thy heavenly kingdom, for to Thee belong glory, power, and dominion, together with Thy Father, who is without beginning, and Thy All-holy, good, and comforting Spirit, both now and ever and to the ages of ages. Amen.

---

* Gal 3:28

† Lev 19:18; Mt 19:19; Mt 22:39; Mk 12:31; cf. Lk 10:27; Rom 13:9; Gal 5:14 & Jas 2:8.

‡ Cf. Phil 4:7

APPENDIX II

FURTHER
INFORMATION

Fellowship of St. Moses the Black
http://mosestheblack.org
info@mosestheblack.org

For sales of the UNBROKEN CIRCLE SERIES books
http://mosestheblack.org/resources/books

Fellowship of St. Moses the Black Annual Conferences
http://mosestheblack.org/conferences

For musical scores and recordings of liturgical music inspired by Spirituals
http://mosestheblack.org/resources/our-music

Holy Resurrection Cemetery, Ash Grove, Missouri
c/o Fr. Moses Berry
14617 West Farm Road #74
Ash Grove, MO 65604
Phone: 417-751-9763

APPENDIX III

RECOMMENDED READING

Hieromonk Alexii Altschul & Nun Macaria Corbett, eds., *Foundations: 1994–1997*. Indianapolis, IN: Unbroken Circle Press, 2021.

Fellowship of St. Moses the Black, *Akathist to the Merciful Savior: Healer of the Wounds of American Slavery*. Indianapolis, IN: Unbroken Circle Press, 2021.

Fr. Paul Abernathy, *The Prayer of a Broken Heart: An Orthodox Christian Reflection on African American Spirituality*. Chesterton, IN: Ancient Faith Publishing, 2022.

Fr. Paisius Altschul, *Wade in the River: The Story of the African Christian Faith*. Kansas City, MO: CrossBearers Publishing, 2001.

Deacon John R. Gresham, Jr., *Become All Flame: Lent with African Saints*. Sugarland, TX: Park End Books, 2022.

Nun Katherine Weston, *Race, Identity, and Reconciliation*, Revised Edition. Indianapolis, IN: Weston Counseling, LLC, Publications, 2017.

NOTES

Introduction: Music of a Suffering People

1 Arthur C. Jones, *Wade in the Water: The Wisdom of the Spirituals,* 3rd edition (Boulder, CO: Leave a Little Room, 2005).

Chapter 1
From the Heart to the Heart:
Matushka Michaila and Gospel Music

1 Archpriest Michael Carney, personal conversation with the author, October 13, 2020.

2 David Drillock and John H. Erickson, eds. *Holy Week,* vol. 3, The Services of Holy Saturday (Crestwood, NY: St. Vladimir's Seminary Press, 2005), 94.

Chapter 2
Singing the Lord's Song:
The Theology of American Slave Spirituals

1 Frederick Douglass, *Narrative Life of Frederick Douglass* (New York: Signet Classics, 2005), 30.

2 W. E. B. Du Bois, *The Souls of Black Folk,* (New York: Dover Publications, 1994), 117.

3 James Cone, *The Spirituals and the Blues,* (New York: Orbis Books, 1991), 4.

4 James Weldon Johnson and Rosamond Johnson, eds., *The Books of American Negro Spirituals,* vol. 1 (New York: The Viking Press, 1969), 62–63.

5 Frances Banks, "Narrative" in *The WPA Oklahoma Slave Narratives,* ed. T. Lindsay Baker & Julie P. Baker (Norman, OK: University of Oklahoma Press, 1996), 28.

6 Frederick Douglass, *My Bondage and My Freedom* (New York: Dover Publications, 1969), 273.

7 William Francis Allen, Charles Pickard Ware and Lucy McKim Garrison, eds., *Slave Songs of the United States,* (Chapel Hill, NC: University of North Carolina at Chapel Hill Library, 2011), 76.

8 Albert J. Raboteau, *Slave Religion: The "Invisible Institution" in the Antebellum South* (New York: Oxford University Press, 1978), 96.

9 Ibid., 123.

10 Douglass, *My Bondage and My Freedom,* 273.

11 Nat Turner, *The Confessions of Nat Turner, the Leader of the Late Insurrection in Southampton, Va.,* ed. Thomas R. Gray (Chapel Hill, NC: The University of North Carolina at Chapel Hill Library, 2011), 20.

12 Ibid., 21.

13 Johnson & Johnson, *The Books of American Negro Spirituals,* vol 1, 115.

14 Lydia Maria Child, "Charity Bowery," *The Liberty Bell by Friends of Freedom* (Boston: American Anti-Slavery Society, 1839), 42.

15 Ibid.

16 Ibid.

17 United States Work Projects Administration, "Federal Writers' Project: Slave Narrative Project, Vol. 2, Arkansas, Part 1, Abbott-Byrd. November–December, 1936," *Library of Congress,* accessed July 1, 2022, https://www.loc.gov/item/mesn021.

18 United States Work Projects Administration, "Federal Writers' Project: Slave Narrative Project, Vol. 11, North Carolina, Part 2, Jackson-Yellerday, 1936," *Library of Congress,* accessed July 1, 2022, https://www.loc.gov/item/mesn112.

19 United States Work Projects Administration, "Federal Writers' Project: Slave Narrative Project, Vol. 3, Florida, Anderson-Wilson with combined interviews of others. 1936," *Library of Congress,* accessed July 1, 2022, https://www.loc.gov/item/mesn030.

[20] Father Paisius Altschul, ed., *An Unbroken Circle: Linking Ancient African Christianity to the African-American Experience* (St. Louis, MO: Brotherhood of St. Moses the Black, 1997), 169–170. [Out of print. See: Hieromonk Alexii Altschul & Nun Macaria Corbett, eds., *Foundations: 1994–1997*, Unbroken Circle Series, vol. 1 (Indianapolis, IN: Unbroken Circle Press, 2021), 199–200].

[21] Howard Thurman, *Deep River: Reflections on the Religious Insight of Certain of the Negro Spirituals* (New York: Harper, 1955), 13.

[22] Ibid.

[23] Ibid., 14.

[24] Theodore the Syncellus, "Theodore the Syncellus, Homily on the siege of Constantinople in 626 AD," *The Tertullian Project*, 2007, https://www.tertullian.org/fathers/theodore_syncellus_01_homily.htm.

[25] Holy Trinity Monastery, *The Unabbreviated Horologion or the Book of the Hours*, 2nd ed. (Jordanville, New York: Print Shop of Saint Job of Pochaev, 2020), 235; *At the Lighting of the Lamps: Hymns of the Ancient Church*, ed. and trans. John Anthony McGuckin (Eugene, OR: Wipf and Stock Publishers, 1995), 24–27.

[26] Johnson & Johnson, *The Books of American Negro Spirituals*, vol 1, 114–117.

[27] Thomas W. Talley, *Negro Folk Rhymes: Wise and Otherwise* (New York: The Macmillan Company, 1922), 301.

[28] Johnson & Johnson, *The Books of American Negro Spirituals*, vol 1, 101–102.

[29] Raboteau, *Slave Religion*, 128–129.

[30] John W. Work, ed., *American Negro Songs and Spirituals: A Comprehensive Collection of 230 Folk Songs, Religious and Secular* (New York: Bonanza Books, 1940), 143.

[31] Allen, et al., *Slave Songs of the United States*, 10.

[32] Johnson & Johnson, *The Books of American Negro Spirituals*, vol 2, 110–113.

[33] Ibid.

[34] Ibid.

[35] Allen, et al., *Slave Songs of the United States*, 135–136.

[36] Johnson & Johnson, *The Books of American Negro Spirituals*, vol 1, 78–79.

[37] Ibid., 39–40.

[38] Thurman, *Deep River*, 44.

[39] Ibid., 20.

[40] Work, *American Negro Songs and Spirituals*, 88.

[41] Holy Trinity Monastery, *The Unabbreviated Horologion or the Book of the Hours*, 2nd ed. (Jordanville, New York: Print Shop of Saint Job of Pochaev, 2020), 380.

42 *The Pentecostarion of the Orthodox Church,* trans. Reader Isaac E. Lambertsen (Liberty, TN: The St. John of Kronstadt Press, 2010), 5.

43 Thurman, *Deep River,* 21.

44 Ibid., 22.

45 Johnson & Johnson, *The Books of American Negro Spirituals,* vol 2, 136.

46 Raboteau, *Slave Religion,* 301–302.

47 Work, *American Negro Songs and Spirituals,* 108.

48 Ibid.

49 Thurman, *Deep River,* 39–40.

50 St. Basil the Great, *Letters and Select Works,* trans. Bloomfield Jackson, Nicene and Post-Nicene Fathers, Series 2, vol. 8 (Grand Rapids: Eerdmans, 1994), 29.73.46.

51 St. Ignatius of Antioch, *Epistle to the Romans,* trans. Alexander Roberts and James Donaldson, Ante-Nicene Fathers, vol. 1 (Buffalo, NY: Christian Literature Publishing Co., 1885), 4:1.

Chapter 3
Calling Down the Holy Spirit: African American Hymnography

1 Dunbar, P.L. *The Complete Poems of Paul Laurence Dunbar* (New York: Dodd, Mead, and Company, 1913).

2 Fr. Damascene Christensen, "The Call of the Righteous Slave Confessors," in *Foundations: 1994–1997* (Indianapolis, IN: Unbroken Circle Press, 2021), 116.

3 Paul Robeson. 1989. *Spirituals/Folksongs/Hymns* Pearl, Pavilion Records, Ltd., E. Sussex, England, compact disc.

4 Stevie Wonder. 1976. "Joy Inside My Tears." Track 12 on *Songs in the Key of Life.* Tamla Records, compact disc.

Chapter 4
Orthodox Patristic Themes in African American
Gospel Songs of the Golden Age

1 St. Thalassius of Libya, "On Love, Self-control, and Life according to the Nous" 2.67, in *The Philokalia,* vol. 2 (London: Faber and Faber, 1981), 316.

2 St. Isaac the Syrian, *Daily Readings with St. Isaac of Syria* (Springfield, IL: Templegate Publishers, 1989), 30.

3 Ibid., 33.

4 St. John Climacus, *The Ladder of Divine Ascent* 7.1 (Boston: Holy Transfiguration Monastery, 1991), 70.

5 Ibid. 7.7, 71.

6 St. Maximus the Confessor, "Various Texts on Theology" 1:40–41, in *The Philokalia*, vol. 2 (London: Faber & Faber, 1981), 172–73.

7 St. Maximus the Confessor, "Four Hundred Texts on Love" 1:70–71, in *The Philokalia*, vol. 2, 60.

8 St. John Climacus, *The Ladder of Divine Ascent* 6.4, 66.

9 St. John Cassian, "On the Eight Vices," in *The Philokalia*, vol. 1 (London: Faber and Faber, 1979), 82.

10 St. Theodoros the Great Ascetic, "A Century of Spiritual Texts" 57–58, in *The Philokalia*, vol. 2 (London: Faber & Faber, 1981), 24–25.

11 The Trumpets of Joy of Aliquippa. 1961. "I Need the Lord to Guide Me."

12 Albert J. Raboteau, *Slave Religion: The "Invisible Institution" in the Antebellum South* (New York: Oxford University Press, 1978), 270.

13 St. John Climacus, *The Ladder of Divine Ascent* 6.4, 66.

Chapter 5
Dorothy Love Coates
and the African American Spiritual Tradition

1 Benedicta Ward, SLG, trans., *The Sayings of the Desert Fathers* (Kalamazoo, MI: Cistercian Publications, 1984), 10.

Chapter 6
The Liturgy is a War Cry: Homily to the Choir

1 St. Sophrony (Sakharov) of Essex, *His Life is Mine* (Yonkers: SVS Press, 1997), 88–89.

2 Ibid.

Chapter 7
American Orthodox Music: Towards a Synthesis

1 Mark Bailey, "Composing Orthodox Liturgical Music in the Contemporary World," in *St. Vladimir's Theological Quarterly*, Vol. 40, #1, 2001, 65.

2 Ibid., 71.

3 Ibid.

4 Ibid., 72.

5 Ibid.

6 Fr. Stephen Freeman, "Mission and Worship—America and the Orthodox," on his blog *Glory to God for All Things,* http://fatherstephen.wordpress.com/2007/11/26/mission-and-worship-america-and-the-orthodox.

7 John and Alan Lomax, *Folk Song U.S.A.* (New York: New American Library, 1947), 410.

8 St. John Climacus, *The Ladder of Divine Ascent* (Boston: Holy Transfiguration Monastery, 1978), 70.

9 Albert Raboteau, "The Legacy of a Suffering Church: The Holiness of American Slaves," in *Foundations: 1994–1997*, Vol. 1 of the Unbroken Circle Series, Hieromonk Alexii Altschul and Nun Macaria Corbett, editors (Indianapolis, IN: Unbroken Circle Press, 2021), 109.

10 Lomax, *Folk Song U.S.A.*, 414.

11 Ibid., viii.

12 Mark Bailey, "Toward a Living Tradition of Liturgical Music in Orthodox America," in *SVTQ*, Vol. 47, #2, 2003, 194.

13 *Editor's note:* see, for example, John MacKay, "The First Years of *Uncle Tom's Cabin* in Russia," in Denise Kohn, Sara Meer, and Emily B. Todd, eds., *Transatlantic Stowe: Harriet Beecher Stowe and European Culture* (Iowa City, IA: University of Iowa Press, 2006).

14 Ken Burns, *The Civil War* (PBS documentary, 1990), Part 1.

15 Dimitri E. Conomos, "A Brief Survey of the History of Byzantine and Post-Byzantine Chant," on *The Divine Music Project*, http://www.stanthonysmonastery.org/music/Index.html.

16 Ibid.

17 Ibid.

18 Alexander Schmemann, "Problems of Orthodoxy in America," in *SVTQ*, Vol. 8, #4, 1964, 181.

19 Freeman, "Mission and Worship," from the comment section.

20 *Editor's note:* see, for example, Michael Oleksa, *Orthodox Alaska: A Theology of Mission* (Crestwood, NY: St. Vladimir's Seminary Press, 1992).

21 Conomos, "A Brief Survey."

22 St. Paisios of Mount Athos, *With Pain and Love for Contemporary Man* (Souroti, Greece: Holy Monastery of the Evangelist John the Theologian, 2006), 391.

23 Athanasios Rakovalis, *Talks with Father Paisios* (Thessaloniki: St. Nikodemos the Hagiorite Publication Society, 2000), 123.

Postscript to Chapter 7

24 Fr. Andrew Wermuth, "American Orthodox Music: Towards a Synthesis," in *By the Waters: Selected Works by Students of St. Tikhon's Orthodox Theological Seminary*, Fall 2008, #7 (New Canaan, PA: St. Tikhon's Seminary Press).

25 From the website https://howsweetthesound.net.

26 Benedict Sheehan, personal communication with the author, January 25, 2022.

27 Fellowship of St. Moses the Black, *Akathist to the Merciful Savior: Healer of the Wounds of American Slavery* (Indianapolis, IN: Unbroken Circle Press, 2021).

28 Robert B. Alter, *The Hebrew Bible: A Translation with Commentary* (New York: W. W. Norton, 2018).

29 Composer Notes on the program for Benedict Sheehan's Liturgy of St. John Chrysostom (2018), https://www.conspirare.org/liturgy-of-st-john-chrysostom.

30 W. E. B. Du Bois, *Darkwater: Voices from Beyond the Veil* (New York: Harcourt, Brace and Howe, 1920), 3.

31 Composer notes for Benedict Sheehan's Liturgy.

32 Ibid.

Chapter 8
A Brief History of Spirituals and Gospel Music

1 William Francis Allen, Charles Pickard Ware, and Lucy McKim Garrison, compilers, *Slave Songs of the United States* (Mineola, NY: Dover, 1867 / 1995).

2 J. B. T. Marsh with supplement by F. J. Loudin, *The Jubilee Singers and Their Songs* (Mineola, NY: Dover, 1892 / 2003). This volume was originally published as *The Story of the Jubilee Singers by J. B. T. Marsh / With Supplement containing an account of their six years' tour around the world, and many new songs / by F. J. Loudin / New Edition, completing one hundred and thirtieth thousand,* originally published by the Cleveland Printing and Publishing Co., Cleveland, O., in 1892.

3 Sandra Jean Graham, "How African American Spirituals Moved From Cotton Fields to Concert Halls," Zocalo Public Square, October 29, 2018, https://www.zocalopublicsquare.org/2018/10/29/african-american-spirituals-moved-cotton-fields-concert-halls/ideas/essay.

4 Mary Frances Armstrong, Helen Wilhelmina Ludlow, and Thomas P. Fenner, *Hampton and Its Students by Two of Its Teachers, with Fifty Cabin and Plantation Songs* (New York: G. P. Putnam's Sons, 1874).

5 Graham, "African American Spirituals."

6 U of SC, "Spirituals and Gospel," ND, https://digital.library.sc.edu/exhibits/southernafricanamericanmusic/spirituals-and-gospel.

7 See the Library of Congress article "African American Gospel," ND, https://www.loc.gov/collections/songs-of-america/articles-and-essays/musical-styles/ritual-and-worship/african-american-gospel.

8 Ibid.

9 The Rev. William B. McClain, pastor of Tindley Temple UMC from 2001–2003. See https://archive.wfn.org/2002/09/msg00277.html.

Chapter 9
Spirituals: A Wellspring for Orthodox Liturgical Music

1 See: Albert J. Raboteau, *Slave Religion: The "Invisible Institution" in the Antebellum South,* (New York: Oxford University Press, 1978). See: Fellowship of St. Moses the Black, *Foundations: 1994–1997,* (Indianapolis, IN: Unbroken Circle Press, 2021). See: Fr. Paul Abernathy, *The Prayer of a Broken Heart: An Orthodox Christian Reflection on African American Spirituality,* (Chesterton, IN: Ancient Faith Publishing, 2022).

2 J. B. T. Marsh, *The Jubilee Singers and Their Songs* (Mineola, NY: Dover Publications, 1892/2003), 156.

3 Nun Macaria Corbett, *St. Nikolai Velimirović, "The New Chrysostom": His Life and Service,* (Indianapolis, IN: St. Xenia Monastic Community, 2018).

4 Fellowship of St. Moses the Black, *Akathist to the Merciful Savior: Healer of the Wounds of American Slavery* (Indianapolis, IN: Unbroken Circle Press, 2021).

5 Fr. Paul Abernathy, *The Prayer of a Broken Heart: An Orthodox Christian Reflection on African American Spirituality* (Chesterton, IN: Ancient Faith Publishing, 2022).

Chapter 11
The Spirit of Orthodoxy Choir:
Reflections on Singing Arrangements from Spirituals

1 John Chrysostom, "Homily on Ozias," in *Patrologia Graeca,* ed. J.-P. Migne (Paris: Migne, 1862). As quoted in Ivan Moody, "The Seraphim Above: Some Perspectives on the Theology of Orthodox Church Music," in *Religions,* 6, no. 2 (February 2015): 350–364, https://doi.org/10.3390/rel6020350.

2 Niceta of Remesiana, "On the Benefit of Psalmody," in William Oliver Strunk *Source Readings in Music History,* vol. 2, Edited by James McKinnon (New York: Norton, 1998). As quoted in Ivan Moody, "The Seraphim Above."

Made in the USA
Las Vegas, NV
26 November 2022